The Faith of St. Paul

The Faith of St. Paul

Transformative Gift of Divine Power

ROY A. HARRISVILLE III

PICKWICK *Publications* · Eugene, Oregon

THE FAITH OF ST. PAUL
Transformative Gift of Divine Power

Pickwick Publications
An Imprint of Wipf and Stock Publishers
199 W. 8th Ave., Suite 3
Eugene, OR 97401

www.wipfandstock.com

PAPERBACK ISBN: 978-1-5326-5783-2
HARDCOVER ISBN: 978-1-5326-5784-9
EBOOK ISBN: 978-1-5326-5785-6

Cataloging-in-Publication data:

Names: Harrisville III, Roy A., author.

Title: The faith of St. Paul : transformative gift of divine power / Roy A. Harrisville III.

Description: Eugene, OR : Pickwick Publications, 2019 | Includes bibliographical references.

Identifiers: ISBN 978-1-5326-5783-2 (paperback) | ISBN 978-1-5326-5784-9 (hardcover) | ISBN 978-1-5326-5785-6 (ebook)

Subjects: LCSH: Paul, the Apostle, Saint. | Bible. Epistles of Paul—Criticism, interpretation, etc. | Bible. Epistles of Paul—Theology.

Classification: LCC BS2651 H18 2019 (print) | LCC BS2651 (ebook)

Manufactured in the U.S.A.   03/13/19

For Dad
δοῦλος Χριστοῦ Ἰησοῦ

Yet, were this faith so portrayed, as if it had such a peculiar force and such mystical (or magical) influence that, however much we ought to regard it, from what we know, merely as historical, it would nonetheless be in a position of improving the whole human being radically (of making a new man out of him) if he just holds on to it and to all the feelings bound with it, then such a faith would have to be regarded as itself imparted and inspired directly by heaven (with and within the historical faith), and everything, the moral constitution of humankind included, would then be reduced to an unconditional decree of God: "He hath mercy on whom he will, and whom he will he *hardeneth*," and this, taken according to the letter, is the *salto mortale* of human reason.

IMMANUEL KANT[1]

What do you have that you did not receive?

1 CORINTHIANS 4:7

But he who is deluded by egoism thinks, "I am the doer."

THE BHAGAVAD GITA[2]

1. Kant, *Religion*, 126–27.
2. 3:27

Contents

Acknowledgments | ix

Abbreviations | x

Introduction | xi

1 Justification by Faith and Participation in Christ | 1

2 The Paradox of Faith | 12

3 Faith as Gift and Yet . . . | 43

4 The Objectified Noun and Human Faith in the Letters of St. Paul | 58

5 Faith as Gift in the Letters of St. Paul | 66

6 Faith as Power in the Letters of St. Paul | 84

7 The Faith of St. Paul | 99

Bibliography | 107

Author Index | 111

Scripture Index | 113

Acknowledgments

This book began as a presentation for the 2015 McDaniel Center Reformation Conference at Gordon-Conwell Theological Seminary in Charlotte, North Carolina, to which I had been invited to speak by Dr. Mary Havens, head of the Lutheran Studies program. My thanks are to her and the participants of the conference who helped sharpen my thoughts.

Thanks are also due to Dr. Arland Hultgren, who read the manuscript and rendered invaluable aid in his insightful comments, and to Dr. James Nestingen, who helped identify sources in Luther's works, and to Dr. Walter Sundberg, for his quick perusal and confirmation that I was on the right track. Thanks also to Dr. Charles Puskas, who graciously supplied many very helpful remarks on the manuscript.

I also wish to thank my brothers and sisters at New Life Lutheran Church in Menomonie, Wisconsin, whose faith and support have sustained me for many years.

Finally, I thank the Lord for my father, Rev. Dr. Roy A. Harrisville, Jr., to whom my debt is immeasurable, and to whom this book is dedicated.

Soli Deo Gloria

Abbreviations

AHD	*American Heritage Dictionary.*
BDAG	*Greek-English Lexicon of the New Testament.*
BDB	*Hebrew and English Lexicon of the Old Testament.*
BDF	*A Greek Grammar of the New Testament.*
L&N	*Greek-English Lexicon of the New Testament Based on Semantic Domains.*
LW	*Luther's Works.*
OCD	*Oxford Classical Dictionary.*
NovT	Novum Testamentum
RSV	Revised Standard Version
NRSV	New Revised Standard Version
ESV	English Standard version
NIV	New International Version
KJV	King James Version
NKJV	New King James Version
LXX	Septuagint

Introduction

As one believes, so one lives. Whatever faith abides in a person's heart and mind will determine how that person lives his or her life. If a person believes with Protagoras that "man is the measure of all things," such a person will approach life from an anthropological point of view. If one believes in a "Higher Power," that person will live from a theological point of view. If one holds that life is a gift, one will live out of gratitude for each day. If one believes that life is the possession of the self, one will live to fulfill one's own desires. Yet, the human being is never so clearly defined as being in one philosophical category or another, but is rather an amalgam of various points of view often struggling with each other for supremacy, producing such a confused personality that rarely is the person capable of clarion identification. The human being is on the way to one or another destination, weaving to and fro and sometimes turning down a completely different path.

How is it possible that one should take another road? Is the human self actually capable of determining its own path and destiny from day to day, hour to hour, minute to minute? Are there not forces beyond one's control that impact the person so dramatically that seemingly apart from one's conscious will the person is forced in a certain direction? The very faith by which one lives may be changed in such circumstances. The old faith may be wiped away by a new reality and the person be faced with a profound alteration of life that did not spring from the self. Can such a thing be possible?

Saul of Tarsus began his religious career as a pharisaic Jew of the first century. He ended his career as Paul, the missionary Christian. Faith was the difference. Though as a young man he had fervently embraced the traditions of his fathers,[1] his faith was changed dramatically through an

---

1. Gal 1:13–14.

encounter with the risen Lord Jesus on the road to Damascus.[2] Saul was neither desirous of nor prepared for the profound change that began in him that day.[3] He was captured by something wholly unexpected. He became enslaved to a faith that compelled[4] him to travel from place to place, suffering privations, persecutions, and imprisonments, all the while proclaiming what he had once despised.

It is this faith that is under investigation here. What was it that changed Saul of Tarsus? Was it a new attitude, a new outlook on life? Perhaps it was a fresh state of mind. Could it have been a decision to which he arrived after much consideration and study? It may have been an emotional state or a point of view, even a new orientation. Is faith something that the human produces after having been confronted with new information? Perhaps faith is a gift that one employs as best one can. Is it evoked or elicited by spiritual encounters? Is it drawn out of a person as though it had been in hiding somewhere in the soul? Is faith something that must be tickled out of the human, or coaxed and cajoled? Is there a limitless supply of faith in each and every person that needs merely to be drilled into as one drills an oil well? Can the well go dry?

The Roman Catholic Church, which is the largest of the Christian denominations, insists in its official Catechism that faith is a human act that cannot be coerced, for to do so would violate the integrity of human personality.[5] It expressly teaches that faith is a free act of the human will.[6]

---

2. Acts 9:1–19; 22:3–21; 26:9–20; 1 Cor 15:8.

3. Stendahl, "Apostle Paul," 80–81.

4. 1 Cor 9:16.

5. "Believing is possible only by grace and the interior helps of the Holy Spirit. But it is no less true that believing is an authentically human act. Trusting in God and cleaving to the truths he has revealed is contrary neither to human freedom nor to human reason. Even in human relations it is not contrary to our dignity to believe what other persons tell us about themselves and their intentions, or to trust their promises (for example, when a man and a woman marry) to share a communion of life with one another. If this is so, still less is it contrary to our dignity to 'yield by faith the full submission of . . . intellect and will to God who reveals,'[26] and to share in an interior communion with him." *Catechism of the Catholic Church*, 154.

6. "To be human, 'man's response to God by faith must be free, and . . . therefore nobody is to be forced to embrace the faith against his will. The act of faith is of its very nature a free act.'[39] 'God calls men to serve him in spirit and in truth. Consequently they are bound to him in conscience, but not coerced. . . . This fact received its fullest manifestation in Christ Jesus.'[40] Indeed, Christ invited people to faith and conversion, but never coerced them." *Catechism of the Catholic Church*, 160.

The genuineness and authenticity of faith must be maintained, so it seems, by regarding faith as a product of human will.

Pope Francis penned an encyclical letter in 2013 entitled LUMEN FIDEI. This letter, which occasionally mentions the faith of St. Paul, deals with what it calls the Light of Faith. This light is a divine gift.[7] Yet, this gift is not to be "taken for granted" and requires some assistance.[8] This "supernatural infused virtue" is to be welcomed and enables people to advance joyfully into the future.[9]

On the other hand, His Holiness emphasizes the human side of faith and writes about persons being open to and recognizing the divine gift of faith.[10] Moreover, faith is definitely a human response to God.[11] It is a human act.[12] Abraham entrusted himself to God by faith.[13] Though faith is a gift, it still "calls for humility and the courage to trust and entrust; it enables

7. "1. The Light of Faith: this is how the Church's tradition speaks of the great gift brought by Jesus." Pope Francis, *LUMEN FIDEI*, 3. "A light this powerful cannot come from ourselves but from a more primordial source: in a word, it must come from God." Pope Francis, *LUMEN FIDEI*, 5–6. "Faith is God's free gift, which calls for humility and the courage to trust and entrust; it enables us to see the luminous path leading to the encounter of God and humanity: the history of salvation." 17. "Faith becomes operative in the Christian on the basis of the gift received, the love which attracts our hearts to Christ (cf. Gal 5:6)." Pope Francis, *LUMEN FIDEI*, 27.

8. "The Church never takes faith for granted, but knows that this gift of God needs to be nourished and reinforced so that it can continue to guide her pilgrim way." Pope Francis, *LUMEN FIDEI*, 8.

9. "In God's gift of faith, a supernatural infused virtue, we realize that a great love has been offered us, a good word has been spoken to us, and that when we welcome that word, Jesus Christ the Word made flesh, the Holy Spirit transforms us, lights up our way to the future and enables us joyfully to advance along that way on wings of hope." Pope Francis, *LUMEN FIDEI*, 9.

10. "The beginning of salvation is openness to something prior to ourselves, to a primordial gift that affirms life and sustains it in being. Only by being open to acknowledging this gift can we be transformed, experience salvation and bear good fruit. Salvation by faith means recognizing the primacy of God's gift." Pope Francis, *LUMEN FIDEI*, 23–24.

11. "Faith is our response to a word which engages us personally, to a 'Thou' who calls us by name." Pope Francis, *LUMEN FIDEI*, 11. "As a response to a word which preceded it, Abraham's faith would always be an act of remembrance." Pope Francis, *LUMEN FIDEI*, 12.

12. "The individual's act of faith finds its place within a community." Pope Francis, *LUMEN FIDEI*, 17.

13. "Abraham is asked to entrust himself to this word." 12. "The God who asks Abraham for complete trust reveals himself to be the source of all life." Pope Francis, *LUMEN FIDEI*, 13.

us to see the luminous path leading to the encounter of God and humanity: the history of salvation."[14] "Faith transforms the whole person precisely to the extent that he or she becomes open to love."[15] It is this human openness that leads to faith.[16]

In a long footnote quotation from Vatican II on pages 36 and 37, His Holiness includes an extended discussion of the Pauline phrase: "obedience of faith" (Rom 1:5; 16:26). This footnote contends that obedience of faith

> must be our response to the God who reveals. By faith one freely submits oneself to God making the full submission of intellect and will to God who reveals, and willingly assenting to the revelation given by God. For this faith to be accorded, we need the grace of God, anticipating it and assisting it, as well as the interior helps of the Holy Spirit, who moves the heart and converts it to God, and opens the eyes of the mind and makes it easy for all to accept and believe the truth. The same Holy Spirit constantly perfects faith by his gifts, so that revelation may be more and more deeply understood (SECOND VATICAN ECUMENICAL COUNCIL, Dogmatic Constitution on Divine Revelation Dei Verbum, 5).[17]

Faith is thus a response or self-submission and willing assent to God. It is a movement of the heart that God and the Holy Spirit anticipate and assist. But it is still the self that submits and assents. It is still one's own heart that moves and responds, albeit with the gracious assistance of the Divine. But if God only assists the heart and will, then he cannot be fully credited with the final product of faith, which must be, at least in part, the product of the human heart and will. Thus, faith, according to Vatican II and Pope Francis, is both a divine and human responsibility.

Yet, such views cause confusion when it comes to the Pauline opposition of faith and works (e.g., Gal 3:1–5; Rom 4:5). If faith is a human act, then it is obviously a human work. But if Paul diametrically opposes faith on the one side and works on the other, how can it be that he understands faith as a human act or work?

How may one understand the expressions of faith in St. Paul's letters? *If* faith is a gift, then how is it that Paul places humans in the position of the

14. Pope Francis, *LUMEN FIDEI*, 17.

15. Pope Francis, *LUMEN FIDEI*, 33.

16. "To the extent that they are sincerely open to love and set out with whatever light they can find, they are already, even without knowing it, on the path leading to faith." Pope Francis, *LUMEN FIDEI*, 47.

17. Pope Francis, *LUMEN FIDEI*, 36–37.

subject of the verb "believe"? How can he write that people actually believe if faith does not derive from the individual? How could an external act of Christ on the cross become an internal reality of the Christian? This leads us to the issue of juridical and existential righteousness, which has been a perennial topic of discussion.[18] Indeed, where faith is concerned there arise numerous difficult dichotomies: mystical versus juridical; ought versus is; objective versus subjective; I versus Thou; old versus new; forensic versus actual; indicative versus the imperative, justification by faith versus participation in Christ. The latter opposition has occupied New Testament scholarship for the last century and has been renewed by the now familiar New Perspective on Paul. I argue that faith is at the center of this debate and that when one deals with faith properly, the debate evaporates.

The present study will focus on the faith of St. Paul in general (including the dilemma of faith as gift and act, and how faith touches on the Πίστις Χριστοῦ issue), and at the same time address the supposed contrast between justification by faith and participation in Christ. The argument here is that the two seemingly discreet theologies encompass the same sentiment. Those who wish to play one of them off the other have made two errors: 1) That "justification by faith" is a purely juridical concept; 2) that "participation in Christ" is separate and superior to justification. Moreover, the concept of participation is often poorly constructed because when that concept is divorced from justification it leaves the Christian with

18. "'Participation' and 'justification' are regularly spoken of as two major and quite different categories of thought in Paul's mind. The relationship between them, historically, theologically and (not least) exegetically remains one of the major questions in the discipline. Since I have argued elsewhere that this dichotomy is fundamentally ill-conceived, and that the two are outworkings of a larger theme which the discipline has not normally recognized or worked with, it is at least important that we recognize how powerfully present within the whole discourse of Pauline studies this distinction has been, and acknowledge the role of Schweitzer in stating so clearly the historical, theological and (in a measure) exegetical problems as they appeared a hundred years ago." Wright, *Paul and His Recent Interpreters*, 37–38. "There are some ways of reading Paul—serious, carefully thought-out ways, not casual let's-hope-it-works ways—in which the antithesis maintained by Schweitzer, Bultmann, Käsemann and, as we shall see, Sanders, Campbell and others has been called into question: the antithesis, that is, between 'being in Christ' on the one hand, expressed either in 'incorporative' or in 'participationist' categories, and 'justification by faith' on the other, expressed in 'juristic,' 'forensic' or 'relational' categories." Wright, *Paul and His Recent Interpreters*, 62. Wright thinks the concept of "covenant" can bridge the gap: "Sanders has seen that what have appeared to some as two separate things are in fact two different angles of vision on the same thing. But he cannot reach out and grasp the category through which they might be finally and satisfyingly reconciled: that is, the covenant." Wright, *Paul and His Recent Interpreters*, 83.

precious little connection to Christ. There only remains a slim ritualistic connection in baptism or an amorphous claim to identification, as with a character in a novel.[19] If those are to be the connections between the deity and the devotee, they are indeed frail because they are merely human, just as the identification of faith as a work is weak because that too is merely human. What assurance does one have of redemption if redemption relies ultimately upon the believer and not the One believed?

N. T. Wright thinks that both Ernst Käsemann and E. P. Sanders correctly wished to keep justification by faith and participation in Christ together in Paul's theology, but did not find an avenue by which to do that.[20] This dilemma is grounded in the old debate concerning "divine sovereignty and human responsibility" both within Judaism and Christianity.[21] Wright thinks he can point the way to solving this dilemma through what he identifies as a "Pauline 'new-covenantal fideism.'"[22] Drawing upon Sanders's work, Wright would also like to expand Sanders's "covenantal nomism" into a "covenantal/nomistic narrative" in an effort to get at this debate because

> until we recognize, name, and flesh out the *narrative* of the covenant, as it was inhabited by many first-century Jews and in particular the Pharisees, all the debate about grace and works, about the exact balance between what God does and what humans do, about how all this contributes to "salvation," will simply go round and round in circles, ending up with a lot more footnotes and a lot less illumination.[23]

The dilemma of how justification by faith relates to participation in Christ cannot be solved by concepts of narrative or covenant. Such concepts are not expansive enough to contain the cosmic significance of St. Paul's theology. They do not carry within them the existential significance necessary to address personal angst over sin and death, or indeed, over apathy to religion.

What if the two concepts of participation and justification were not only linked, but the very same thing? What if participation in Christ *is* justification by faith in Christ? Then Paul's theology becomes a unified whole

---

19. Hays, *Faith of Jesus Christ*, 214.

20. Wright, *Paul and His Recent Interpreters*, 84.

21. Wright, *Paul and His Recent Interpreters*, 109.

22. Wright, *Paul and His Recent Interpreters*, 85.

23. Wright, *Paul and His Recent Interpreters*, 111.

in which participation and justification language both address the entire life of the believer.

This way of reading St. Paul effectively addresses the opposition between the so-called New Perspective and the traditional Reformation theology. It also renders moot the Πίστις Χριστοῦ issue, since if faith is a gift in Paul's theology then there is no need to employ a novel solution to the juxtaposition of the works of the law and hearing of faith.[24] In addition, it answers the conundrum of how one may be the subject of believing while at the same time insisting that faith is not a human work. The faith of St. Paul is far more organic than has been expressed by scholars over the years and it is this organic nature that overcomes a number of obstacles to properly understanding that faith.

When one reads St. Paul, one must not blithely assume that he is expounding a mere philosophy of faith to be debated among scholars or to be commented upon by priests and ministers. Rather, this is a faith of immediate and immense power and significance. It is a force capable of moving mountains.[25] Faith means to enter the heart and, as Immanuel Kant remarked, to change the person "from the ground up" until the person cannot conceive of another thought, another hope, or another life.[26] By faith the person becomes a completely new person.

Is faith, then, a product of the human will or a gift of God, or both? The manner in which the question is answered will determine the direction of one's theology (and whether justification by faith is the center of Pauline theology or not). Often the answer is assumed and never debated within scholars' works. Yet, it is a foundational issue that cannot be passed over since upon it rests the answer to how a person understands redemption. It is vital therefore that we first investigate what scholars have been saying about the faith of St. Paul and how the divide between participation in Christ and justification by faith language arose so that we may gain a clear picture of why the debates about Pauline theology have taken the shape they have and raised the questions they do.

24. Hays, *Faith of Jesus Christ*, 130.

25. 1 Cor 13:2.

26. ". . .von Grunde aus. . ." Kant, *Die Religion*, 111.

1

Justification by Faith
and Participation in Christ

THE DIFFICULTY OF DESCRIBING the faith of St. Paul and explaining the connection between the believer and the Believed has occupied Christian scholars for generations. The dilemma manifested itself in different forms over the centuries, but today it finds expression in the debate between those who embrace the Reformation formula of "justification by faith" on the one hand, and on the other hand, those who espouse the formula: "participation in Christ." The two camps, characterized as the Lutheran/Reformed Perspective and the New Perspective on Paul, are often talking past each other, sometimes even ignoring each other. They seem to be crystallizing into entrenched positions that cause a serious division in the church and theological scholarship. Each side wants to triumph over the other by producing ever more sophisticated and arcane arguments that they hope will crush the opposition. This state of affairs has arisen over a number of years and warrants investigation.

E. P. Sanders has been responsible in large measure for the direction of Pauline studies in recent years beginning with his influential book, *Paul and Palestinian Judaism*.[1] This book reflects the point of view of faith as a human work, which we encountered in the introduction. Sanders writes that although St. Paul's message was "not about man and does not describe

---

1. Sanders, *Paul and Palestinian Judaism*.

1

him, it is intended to elicit 'faith,' and faith can only be individual."[2] He considers faith as decision, acceptance, and response to the gospel.[3] "'Faith' alone, in a way, *is* a prerequisite, since it signifies conversion and being Christian: the Spirit is received by believing the gospel message."[4] Clearly, Sanders considers faith a human work if it is the prerequisite to receiving the Spirit. If faith is elicited, or drawn out, it must have had a prior existence within the individual and needed to be extracted from the person. Does Sanders regard faith as a capacity innate within the person that requires the right catalyst to bring it forth?

Sanders, moreover, states that the doctrine of "righteousness by faith" receives little development from St. Paul and that this teaching does not lead to ethics, neither does it help explain the importance of the sacraments, nor the gift of the Spirit, and "it does not account for the participatory soteriology which we have already discussed."[5] He derives such views from Albert Schweitzer, whose work is discussed below.

In *Paul, the Law, and the Jewish People* Sanders portrays Pauline faith as an entrance requirement.[6] The opposition between faith and law in Paul's letters has more to do "with the central membership requirement, rather than with a whole way of life."[7]

Moreover, according to Sanders, there is actually no real opposition between faith and works. In the letter to the Galatians,

> Neither of the opposing factions saw the requirements of "doing" to be a denial of faith. When Paul makes requirements of his converts, he does not think that he has denied faith, and there is no reason to think that Jewish Christians who specified different

---

2. Sanders, *Paul and Palestinian Judaism*, 446.

3. "When he has in mind the human need for decision for Christ's lordship, the terminology is that of 'faith.'" Sanders, *Paul and Palestinian Judaism*, 447. "In Rom. 3.25, for example . . . 'faith' means accepting the gratuity of salvation." Sanders, *Paul and Palestinian Judaism,* 490. "Faith represents man's entire response to the salvation offered in Jesus Christ, apart from law; and the argument for faith is really an argument against the law." Sanders, *Paul and Palestinian Judaism*, 491.

4. Sanders, *Paul and Palestinian Judaism*, 492.

5. Sanders, *Paul and Palestinian Judaism*, 492.

6. "Paul holds that faith is the sole membership requirement; his opponents would require also circumcision and acceptance of the Mosaic law." Sanders, *Paul, the Law*, 20.

7. Sanders, *Paul, the Law*, 159.

requirements denied faith. The supposed conflict between "doing" as such and "faith" as such is simply not present in Galatians.[8]

Further, "when faith is seen as not being the opposite of "good works" in and of themselves, there will be less pressure to think that Paul accused Judaism *of* good works—of legalism and reliance on self-achievement."[9] Dr. Sanders regards faith as an action that even Apostles must "do": "Even Peter and Paul, who had lived as righteous Jews, had to do something else to be members of the people of God; they had to have faith in Christ (Gal. 2:15f.)."

Sanders's interpretation of Pauline faith is that of an entrance requirement that one must perform. Faith is a "doing" for Sanders that is not essentially opposed to works, and that is why he does not see much difference between Paul's Christianity and his former life in Judaism. The only difference he finds between the two religions is that one of them lacks Christ.[10] Thus, for Sanders, Christianity is not essentially different from Judaism, except for the novelty of Jesus.

If that is so, then why does the Apostle spend so much time and energy and risk the good will, especially of the Galatians, to argue so strenuously for his faith in the way he does? Why did he endure such hardships and privations if only for a novel addition to his old life? That Christ is the essential difference between Christianity and all other religions is obvious, but what is not so obvious is what the difference actually means in the life of the believer. Christ is not a mere addition onto one's already adequate devotion. He is not a spice to be added to the dish. Rather, he is the essential difference that makes a person into a new creature altogether.[11]

From Sanders's understanding of faith springs the assertion that "justification by faith" must not be the central doctrine of Paul's theology, but rather the central teaching of the Apostle is a participation in Christ. This view is reflected in a recent interview that Richard B. Hays had with E. P. Sanders, which was subsequently published.[12] Hays introduces the interview by remarking

---

8. Sanders, *Paul, the Law*, 159.

9. Sanders, *Paul, the Law*, 159.

10. "I have elsewhere written that his real attack on Judaism is against the idea of the covenant and that what he finds wrong in Judaism is that it lacks Christ." Sanders, *Paul, the Law*, 47.

11. Gal 6:15.

12. Hays, "What Is 'Real Participation'?," 336–51.

One of the principal contributions of E. P. Sanders's *Paul and Palestinian Judaism* was its rigorous argument that "the main theme of Paul's theology is found in his participationist language rather than in the theme of righteousness by faith." That is to say, Paul's soteriology focuses on themes of union with Christ rather than on juridical conceptions of atonement." In contending for this position, Sanders was, of course, recovering and refining a central thesis of Albert Schweitzer's *The Mysticism of Paul the Apostle*.[13]

By describing "righteousness by faith" as a "juridical" concept Hays implies that it is a distant and disconnected determination, whereas "participationist language" describes a union with Christ that is more immediate and actual. Intriguingly however, Hays notes that Sanders considered righteousness by faith and participation in Christ as ultimately amounting to the same thing.[14] Yet, there exists in Sanders's thinking a deep divide between righteousness by faith and participation in Christ partly because of Albert Schweitzer's observation that ethics cannot be derived from the doctrine of righteousness by faith. "Paul, however, never made an argument which would bridge the gap between being justified and ethics."[15]

Hays attempts to explain how one may participate in Christ by suggesting four different proposals including: 1) Belonging to a Family; 2) Political or Military Solidarity with Christ; 3) Participation in the Church; and 4) Living within the Christ Story.[16] He concludes that Eastern Orthodoxy may also help with its emphases on meditation, imitation, and contemplative prayer.[17]

In the article following that of Hays, Stanley K. Stowers attempts to answer the question of how participation in Christ actually leads to ethics.[18] Stowers claims that Schweitzer "never tells us how the idea of one person being in another person or sharing in the experiences of another would make sense to Paul or to others in his culture."[19] "We seem to lack a category of "reality"—real participation in Christ, real possession of the Spirit—which lies between naïve cosmological speculation and belief in

13. Hays, "What Is 'Real Participation'?," 336.

14. Hays, "What Is 'Real Participation'?," 337. See also Sanders, *Paul and Palestinian Judaism*, 506.

15. Sanders, *Paul and Palestinian Judaism*, 439.

16. Hays, "What Is 'Real Participation'?," 339–47.

17. Hays, "What Is 'Real Participation'?," 348.

18. Stowers, "What Is 'Pauline Participation'?," 352–71.

19. Stowers, "What Is 'Pauline Participation'?," 353.

magic transference on the one hand and a revised self understanding on the other."[20] Since he also has difficulty with Richard Hays's proposals, Stowers suggests a scheme that involves a more spiritual yet substantive approach. "One simply cannot understand Paul's idea of participation without recognizing that those who are in or of Christ actually possess as part of them the stuff of Christ, a portion of his pneuma."[21] This spiritual substance grants people material improvement, forgiveness of past sins, and empowers and fills them "with a holy stuff that actively enables obedience to God."[22]

In an effort to try and answer the problem of the relationship between participation in Christ and ethics, John M. G. Barclay suggests in the next and final article that there is a interplay between divine and human agency and that grace is not simply a one-time gift but continuous, which enables one to do good works.[23] He writes of a "dual agency of God/grace and believers" that is not "simply one of "gift and response," since the grace that provokes the believer's action continues to be active in that "response" and is not simply its motivation or inspiration."[24] Barclay writes of the self that has been transformed into one capable of agency, but an agency that is "embedded within the agency of divine grace."[25] As close as Barclay comes to a solution to the problem, he is nevertheless at a loss to explain how the good deeds of the person are "the product of the gracious and transformative union with Christ."[26]

As Hays pointed out concerning Sanders's understanding of Pauline soteriology, he was only recovering and refining an older thesis from a famous theologian of the past. In order to understand the modern division between justification and participation it is vital that we study not only the scholar whom Hay's mentions, but two of his predecessors as well.

For the last century Albert Schweitzer's, *The Mysticism of Paul the Apostle,* has enjoyed a celebrated place within the halls of Pauline theology.[27] Schweitzer asserts that the center of Pauline thought was not the doctrine of righteousness by faith, but rather a being-in-Christ that places

---

20. Stowers, "What Is 'Pauline Participation'?," 354.

21. Stowers, "What Is 'Pauline Participation'?," 362.

22. Stowers, "What Is 'Pauline Participation'?," 365.

23. Barclay, "Grace and the Transformation," 372–89.

24. Barclay, "Grace and the Transformation," 384.

25. Barclay, "Grace and the Transformation," 384.

26. Barclay, "Grace and the Transformation," 386.

27. Schweitzer, *Mysticism.*

one in a mystical relationship with the Savior by virtue of baptism.[28] He understands faith as an act of the individual.[29] It is an appropriation of the mind.[30] Christ's accomplishments are appropriated through belief "which is man's necessary part."[31] Concerning present day faith, Schweitzer writes that "the ardour of the early days of the Christian faith kindles our own."[32]

Schweitzer places a great deal of emphasis upon baptism as the crucial act that places one within the Being-in-Christ and not the act of faith.[33] Yet, Schweitzer seems to say that one must, by virtue of one's own resolve, be

28. "This 'being-in-Christ' is the prime enigma of the Pauline teaching: once grasped it gives the clue to the whole." Schweitzer, *Mysticism*, 3. "The original and central idea of the Pauline Mysticism is therefore that the Elect share with one another and with Christ a corporeity which is in a special way susceptible to the action of the powers of death and resurrection, and in consequence capable of acquiring the resurrection state of existence before the general resurrection of the dead takes place . . . that inclusion in this favoured corporeity is not effected in the moment of believing, and not by faith as such. It is first by Baptism, that is, by the ceremonial act by which the believer enters the 'Community of God' and comes into fellowship, not only with Christ, but also with the rest of the Elect, that this inclusion takes place." Schweitzer, *Mysticism*, 115–16.

29. "The most important thing for him is . . . that in this way it is possible for him to give an intelligible form to the conception of a righteousness which results from the action [Leistung] of faith . . . and makes believers Abraham's seed purely by their act [Tat] of faith." Schweitzer, *Mysticism*, 218. German original taken from Schweitzer, *Die Mystik*, 213–14.

30. "There is a series of facts which suggest that the doctrine of the redemption which is mentally appropriated through faith, is only a fragment from the more comprehensive mystical redemption-doctrine, which Paul has broken off and polished to give him the particular refraction which he requires." Schweitzer, *Mysticism*, 220. See also, "we ourselves do not think of redemption as something quasi-physical, but as consisting in the intellectual appropriation of what Christ is for us." Schweitzer, *Mysticism*, 219. "And, moreover, they overlooked the fact that, however it may suit our taste to represent the results of Jesus' death as appropriated by the mind, there clings to it something alien to our thought." Schweitzer, *Mysticism*, 220.

31. Schweitzer, *Mysticism*, 289.

32. Schweitzer, *Mysticism*, 396.

33. "In the Hellenistic mysticism the believer lives on the store of experience which he acquired in the initiation. With Paul, his whole being, from his baptism onwards, is a constantly renewed experiencing of the dying and rising again which began in that act." Schweitzer, *Mysticism*, 16–17. "He [Paul] simply asserts that it is Baptism that the being-in-Christ and the dying and rising again have their beginning." Schweitzer, *Mysticism*, 19. "The idea that it is only through a believing self-surrender to absorption in Christ that the Elect can bring about the mystical fellowship with Him is quite outside of Paul's horizon. He assumes as self-evident that a grafting into Christ takes place in Baptism and is bound up with this ceremonial act." Schweitzer, *Mysticism*, 19.

earnest about being in the Spirit (which is the same as being-in-Christ).[34] One may, by accepting the preaching of Christ, enter into the circle of the elect.[35] But one assumes that any such resolve and acceptance must have arisen first out of baptism or incorporation into Christ.[36]

Schweitzer's view of faith prevents him from conceiving of righteousness by faith as anything more than a juridical doctrine, one that is only constructed for the purpose of refuting righteousness by works.[37] He views faith as incapable of resulting in anything but a distant pronouncement of acquittal.[38] Indeed, for Schweitzer, the doctrine of righteousness by faith is unable to stand on its own.[39]

Schweitzer writes that until his time all attempts to derive the being-in-Christ from belief in Christ have failed and that "being-in-Christ is not a subjective experience brought about by a special effort of faith on the part of the believer, but something which happens, in him as in others, at baptism."[40]

---

34. "Being in the Spirit, it rests with the believer to decide whether he will be in earnest about it, and consistently live in the Spirit. He must resolve to let the Spirit rule completely in all his thought, speech, and action." Schweitzer, *Mysticism*, 168.

35. "Those, however, who do not yet belong to the Elect, and in view of their outward conduct must obviously be considered as reprobate, can by accepting his preaching, confirmed as it is by miracle, enter into the rights of elect persons." Schweitzer, *Mysticism*, 180.

36. "All attempts hitherto undertaken to pass from the concept of belief in Christ to that of being-in-Christ have proved a failure; and all that may be made in the future are equally without prospect of success. They all come to the same point, that the belief in Christ, growing in depth, is by verbal ingenuity made to figure as a being-in-Christ. That the being-in-Christ arises out of such an enhancement of belief in Christ is nowhere indicated by Paul and is nowhere presupposed by him." Schweitzer, *Mysticism*, 116–17.

37. Schweitzer, *Mysticism*, 25.

38. "That righteousness comes directly from faith cannot be meant by Paul in the strict sense, since it is in fact impossible. All the blessings of redemption which the believer possesses flow from the being-in-Christ, and from this only. Faith, in the abstract, has no effective significance: it becomes operative only through that being-in-Christ, beginning at baptism, to which it leads." Schweitzer, *Mysticism*, 206. See n. 36 above.

39. Schweitzer, *Mysticism*, 226.

40. "The peculiarity of the Pauline mysticism is precisely that being-in-Christ is not a subjective experience brought about by a special effort of faith on the part of the believer, but something which happens, in him as in others, at baptism." Schweitzer, *Mysticism*, 117.

Schweitzer further claims that the doctrine of righteousness by faith does not result in other important Pauline doctrines such as redemption, ethics, etc.

> Another point, which tells strongly in favour of the doctrine of righteousness by faith being merely a fragment of a doctrine of redemption, is that Paul does not bring into connection with it the other blessings of redemption, the possession of the spirit, and the resurrection. . . . Neither in seeking a basis for ethics, nor in the doctrines of baptism and the Lord's Supper, does he have recourse to it in any way. In the doctrine of righteousness by faith, his thought is limited to the fact that the believer is justified by the atoning death of Jesus, without finding a way from that fact and the other facts of redemption. The doctrine of redemption can only be developed as a whole from the mystical doctrine of the being-in-Christ.[41]

Schweitzer considers righteousness by faith to be an external action that has no actual impact upon the essence of the person. "[B]ut according to the doctrine of faith-righteousness all that Christ does to believers is to cause them to be justified."[42] He hints at the reason for this judgment on p. 74 where he writes that the eschatological doctrine of redemption is inferior to eschatological mysticism because the former is merely an external interpretation of Christ whereas the latter is an internal interpretation. What he

---

41. Schweitzer, *Mysticism*, 220–21. "Since Paul habitually thinks of redemption on the lines of the mystical doctrine of the being-in-Christ, it does not matter to him that in the subsidiary doctrine of righteousness by faith he has shut off the road to ethics. What he wants this subsidiary doctrine for is to enable him, on the basis of the traditional conception of the atoning death of Christ, to conduct his controversy with the Law by means of the argument from Scripture. More he does not ask of it. But those who subsequently made his doctrine of justification by faith the centre of Christian belief, have had the tragic experience of finding that they were dealing with a conception of redemption, from which no ethic could logically be derived." Schweitzer, *Mysticism*, 225. "Of his two doctrines of righteousness, it is only with the mystical being-in-Christ that Paul brings his ethic into connection; he never makes any attempt to derive it from the righteousness by faith. . . . He might have made for this purpose of the natural demand that the righteousness obtained without works must manifest itself in works. But it would have been difficult to offer proof that it is capable of doing this, or that it carries in itself any impulse in that direction. It would have been necessary to show how the man who previously was inherently incapable of producing good works received through the act of justification the capacity to do so. That capacity can only be bestowed upon him through Christ; but according to the doctrine of faith-righteousness all that Christ does to believers is to cause them to be justified." Schweitzer, *Mysticism*, 294–95.

42. Schweitzer, *Mysticism*, 295.

seems to convey is that an external pronouncement of acquittal (that is how Schweitzer understands righteousness by faith) is not enough to carry the weight of St. Paul's intimate and very personal theology. He searches for a deeper impact on the person, one that redefines and recreates the person. He finds that in the Being-in-Christ doctrine, which he understands to be much more transformative of the individual.

Schweitzer seems to think that faith is a product of the human intellect. Because he says that it can be kindled it therefore stands to reason that in Schweitzer's mind, faith lies dormant or the wherewithal for faith is somehow already present within the person until enflamed by exterior ignition. Faith is part of a juridical concept and is never fully argued by Schweitzer but rather he seems to assume that his readers and he are on the same page with respect to the concept of Christian belief. When he assumes faith is a product of the human mind he is therefore led to the conclusion that righteousness by faith cannot be the central concept of St. Paul's theology but must be an ancillary concept alongside the main concept of Being-in-Christ. In a now famous sentence Schweitzer declared that "The doctrine of righteousness by faith is therefore a subsidiary crater, which has formed within the rim of the main crater—the mystical doctrine of redemption through the Being-in-Christ."[43] It is only because he could not conceive of faith as anything more than intellectual assent that he was prevented from realizing the dynamic character of faith. This is why he searches for a more vibrant theological concept that can incorporate all the complexities of Pauline thought without having to resort to, as he sees it, a mere juridical pronouncement that is dependent upon human effort.

Schweitzer maintains that the Reformers and their successors had difficulty uniting ethics with the doctrine of redemption.[44] Schweitzer's solution is to emphasize that for Paul being-in-Christ was the main point and from that concept neatly flow all the other Pauline teachings. But in his fervor to solve this problem he has created (or rather assumed) another— that faith is not capable of accomplishing righteousness and therefore when the Apostle says that believers are righteous by faith, he cannot mean what he writes![45] Thus, Schweitzer is largely responsible for the separation of righteousness by faith and being-in-Christ because he could not conceive of faith as anything more than a movement of the human will.

43. Schweitzer, *Mysticism,* 225.

44. Schweitzer, *Mysticism,* 393.

45. See n. 38 above.

Albert Schweitzer was not the first to publish on the concept of being-in-Christ. Wilhelm Bousset and Adolf Deissmann both published works a decade before Schweitzer's work appeared. Indeed, both scholars also characterize the Apostle Paul as a mystic.[46]

Deissmann published his *Die neutestamentliche Formel "in Christo Jesu"* in 1892. His *St. Paul: A Study in Social and Religious History* appeared in 1912. He declared that "What St. Paul is, he is in Christ."[47] Wilhelm Bousset published his *Kyrios Christos: A History of the Belief in Christ from the Beginnings of Christianity to Irenaeus* in 1913. He stated, "Thus for Paul Christ becomes the supra-terrestrial power which supports and fills with its presence his whole life. And this Christ piety of the apostle is summed up for him in the one great ever recurring formula of ἐν κυρίω (Χριστῶ) εἶναι."[48] Whereas Deissmann regarded the faith of which the Apostle wrote as union with God,[49] Bousset did not characterize Paul's faith because he thought Paul was not interested in defining it, only in its worth.[50] Bousset considered faith as "firm conviction" and "agreement to a formulated confession."[51] Faith is the "organ" that "grasps the present reality of the πνεῦμα κύριος."[52] Yet, he can also characterize faith as "a previously unheard-of energy."[53] "Nowhere may we forget that behind the personal piety of Paul and his theology there stands as a real power and a living reality the cultic veneration of the κύριος in the community."[54]

Deissmann also regarded faith as energy. "To designate this abundant 'power of Christ,' which streamed through him and took effect from him, St. Paul employed a well-known technical religious term, the Greek word

---

46. Deissmann, *St. Paul*. Bousset, *Kyrios Christos*. "St. Paul has become known to us from the undoubtedly 'genuine' letters as the great mystic where Christ is concerned." Deissmann, *St. Paul*, 23. "Behind Paul's mysticism of the ἐν Χριστῶ εἶναι there stands the living experience of the Kyrios Christos present in worship and in the practical life of the community." Bousset, *Kyrios Christos*, 156.

47. Deissmann, *St. Paul*, 3.

48. Bousset, *Kyrios Christos*, 154.

49. Deissmann, *St. Paul*, 143.

50. Bousset, *Kyrios Christos*, 204.

51. Bousset, *Kyrios Christos*, 203, 205.

52. Bousset, *Kyrios Christos*, 205.

53. Bousset, *Kyrios Christos*, 204.

54. Bousset, *Kyrios Christos*, 210.

pistis, which we are accustomed to translate as 'faith.'"[55] For Deissmann, faith was not a human product but a "divine influence":

> Faith according to Paul is not a human performance before God, but a divine influence upon man in Christ, and justification "out of" faith or "through" faith is in fact justification "in" faith, justification "in Christ," justification "in the name of the Lord Jesus Christ," justification "in His blood." Faith is not the condition precedent to justification, it is the experience of justification.[56]

Albert Schweitzer could not regard justification by faith as the center of Paul's theology because of his lack of regard for faith. Deissmann, on the other hand, seems to be able to hold the two together in a powerful manner, while Bousset does not even deal with the issue. Yet, all three men emphasize the concept of "being-in-Christ" as crucial to understanding the Apostle's theology. Let us accept that Being-in-Christ or participation in Christ is a vital part of St. Paul's theology. How then shall we reconcile righteousness/justification by faith and participation in Christ and provide a more coherent understanding of the Apostle's theology?

As we will discover in the subsequent pages there has been no lack of confusion over what St. Paul meant by faith and how that faith impacted, collided, was subordinate to, or equaled Being-in-Christ. A survey of scholars will demonstrate that the main issue has to do with the dual nature of faith as divine and human. This is vital to the Christian for understanding one's own devotion and how that devotion arises and what it means in a person's life. If one is to look to New Testament scholars over the last 100 years for guidance on the issue, one will have to navigate a maze of theological complexity. In the scholars we will investigate we will encounter time and again the theme of faith as weak and inadequate, baptism as more crucial, and being-in-Christ or participation in Christ as a more suitable doctrine capable of carrying Paul's theological center far better than righteousness by faith. Other scholars will hold up faith as dynamic and wholly adequate for redemption, while at the same time insisting it is a human act. We must investigate both views before we may suggest a solution.

55. Deissmann, *St. Paul,* 139.
56. Deissmann, *St. Paul,* 146–47.

2

The Paradox of Faith

IT MAY BE THE language of the Apostle himself, or it may be the unchallenged assumptions of scholars, or both, that leads us to a paradox of faith. Many assume, following Schweitzer and Sanders, that faith is a human work. However, at the same time these same scholars adamantly insist that faith is not to be considered a meritorious work in any fashion whatsoever. A number of influential scholars have expressed themselves in these terms. The paradox is often left to stand without explanation.

Wilhelm Mundle was convinced that the key to understanding faith in the letters of St. Paul lay in its connection with baptism.[1] Far from fashioning an independent believer, faith ties one to a community of believers. This faith is an act of obedience to God, Christ, and the gospel.[2] Though this human act of obedience cannot be considered a work of the law, it is nonetheless an "achievement" (die menschlicher Leistung) of the human being since, according to Mundle, St. Paul does not discount every human work, only that which is done to keep the Mosaic Law.[3] The idea, writes

---

1. "Der Glaube an Jesus ist das eigentlich charakteristische Kennzeichen der christlichen Gemeinde; an Jesus glauben heißt nicht nur die Botschaft des Evangeliums annehmen, sondern auch sich taufen lassen und ein Glied der Gemeinde werden oder sein." Mundle, *Glaubensbegriff,* 79.

2. "Der paulinische Glaube ist, sofern er als ein Akt des Gehorsams betrachtet werden kann, nicht nur ein Akt des Gehorsams gegen das Evangelium, sondern seiner letzten Intention nach ein Gehorsamkeit gegen Gott oder Christus, den bzw. die letzten Urheber des Gottes- und Christusevangeliums." Mundle, *Glaubensbegriff,* 73.

3. "Aber dadurch wird die Tatsache nicht aufgehoben, daß es sich bei der paulinischen

Mundle, that faith cannot contain an element of "human activity" (*die Selbsttätigkeit*) within St. Paul's theology must be rejected.[4]

Mundle, therefore, is of two minds on the subject of faith. On the one hand, it cannot be considered a work of the law, but on the other hand, it is, partially at least, an achievement of the human being.

However that may be, any "achievement" of humans must be regarded, theologically, as fulfillment of the law, albeit partial. If the human is to be credited, even in small measure, for any religious accomplishment, it can therefore become a ground of boasting. But such boasting is excluded from St. Paul's theology.[5] Yet, when one reads the Apostle's correspondence, an apparent discrepancy emerges when one encounters both the language of grace and that of human acting. Paul insists that man has no boast before God, but at the same time he can write "we have believed,"[6] indicating that humans are the subjects of believing. As such, it could be accepted as fulfilment of the First Commandment, which demands faith. Does the Apostle Paul regard faith as partial fulfillment of the First Commandment, while at the same time insisting that any human work or achievement cannot satisfy the law? If Mundle is confused, perhaps it is only because St. Paul's language has caused the confusion.

Rudolf Bultmann disagreed with Mundle's idea of a Pauline faith that contained "human activity" (*die Selbsttätigkeit*),[7] but he nonetheless was trapped in a similar dilemma. Bultmann describes St. Paul's understanding of faith as "Acceptance of the Kerygma, ὁμολογία and ὑπακοή."[8] He also insists that the decision of faith is not a "work" but constitutes a self-negation. "If one does not understand the paradox that πίστις as a movement of the will is the negation of the will itself, the antithesis of πίστις and ἔργα νόμου will easily be misunderstood, as though πίστις were another

---

Antithese gegen die Gesetzeswerke nicht um den Protest gegen jede Art „menschlicher Leistung, durch die man sich etwas beschaffen und verdienen könnte", handelt, sondern um den sehr viel konkreteren Gegensatz gegen das mosaische Gesetz mit seinen Forderungen." Mundle, *Glaubensbegriff*, 99–100.

4. "Demnach ist die Reflexion, daß der Begriff des Glaubens, wie wir ihn bei Paulus festgestellt haben, auch als ein Werk, eine menschliche Leistung bezeichnet werden müsse, weil er ein Minimum menschlicher Selbsttätigkeit voraussetze, als unpaulinische abzuweisen." Mundle, *Glaubensbegriff*, 100–101.

5. Rom 3:27.

6 . . . καὶ ἡμεῖς εἰς Χριστόν Ἰησοῦν ἐπιστεύσαμεν. Gal 2:16.

7. Schliesser, *Abraham's Faith in Romans 4*, 36.

8. Bultmann, πιστεύω, 217.

work or achievement."[9] On the same page he adds that "the act of faith consists in the negation of all the work which establishes man's existence."[10] However, Bultmann can also say that St. Paul "never describes faith as inspired. Though the Spirit is given to the believer, πίστις is not a gift of the Spirit."[11]

Thus, Bultmann, like Mundle, is caught in a paradox of regarding faith as a human act, yet one which merits no spiritual consideration and is even self-negating. One might therefore consider Bultmann's concept of Pauline faith as spiritual suicide. Though he is clear that the "act" (*die Tat*) of faith occasions no merit whatsoever, and though he studiously refuses to call that "act" a spiritual "work" (*das Werk*), still the description of the event of faith as human "act" can easily be understood as meritorious, for it is the human being who performs the act. It is the person who believes and so negates the very will that "acted" faith. Couple this with the description of faith as "acceptance" and "obedience" and Bultmann becomes trapped in the same quagmire as Mundle, for once again it is the human being doing the accepting and obeying but which accounts for no spiritual merit. Such activity may count for nothing in Bultmann's universe but to insist that a purely human act of deep spiritual significance is worth nothing defies common sense.

When Bultmann writes that faith must "establish itself continually against assaults as an attitude which controls all life" and that "being a Christian is a constant self-relating to God's act of salvation"[12] he means that faith is not merely a single act within time but a continual series of repetitive acts. Thus, for Bultmann, Christian faith is an incessant responsibility of the human. But who can claim responsibility for such a recurrent act of faith of ultimate spiritual significance? Where is the person with such monumental, moral, ethical, and spiritual strength of character as to be forever watchful and courageous enough to maintain faith in a crucified commoner from a backwater province of a dead empire? If Bultmann wishes to express his understanding of faith as a non-meritorious spiritual act of ultimate significance, he will need a vocabulary that makes clear how

---

9. Bultmann, πιστεύω, 220.

10. Also, "Faith is act in the supreme sense. As such it is the opposite of every work of achievement, since the act of faith consists in the negation of all the work which establishes man's existence." Bultmann, πιστεύω, 220.

11. Bultmann, πιστεύω, 219.

12. Bultmann, πιστεύω, 218.

one can say "I believe" and at the same time confess that such belief is no responsibility of the self, but rather represents something divine. This is what Bultmann wishes to convey, but his description of Paul's faith, though an improvement from that of Mundle, needs further revision.

Gerhard Barth, in his article on πίστις in the *Exegetisches Wörterbuch zum Neuen Testament,* describes the faith of St. Paul as "acceptance" (*die Annahme*) and "response" (*die Antwort*).[13]Yet, as with Mundle and Bultmann, he insists that faith is not an achievement. Barth declares that, unlike Judaism, faith is not a virtue or a service and does not take into account its own possibilities or achievements.[14] Faith lives out of the Word but is the corresponding answer of people.[15] Thus, Barth is caught in our now familiar dilemma. Though Pauline faith is not to be understood as a spiritual accomplishment, yet it is something that springs from the individual. It is not an achievement of the person, but it is still the response that comes from the person.

In 1983 a collection of ecumenical theologians met in Rome to discuss "The Apostolic Faith in the Scriptures and in the Early Church." They produced a volume edited by Hans-Georg Link entitled "The Roots of Our Common Faith," which contains a section by Günther Wagner on the faith of St. Paul.[16] In that section Wagner points out that St. Paul does not define faith, nor does he identify it as a virtue or an attitude.[17] Wagner, however, describes Paul's faith in a very familiar way as an "act," an "acceptance," and an "exercise."[18] Hearing the gospel "evokes" faith.[19] Faith has its origin in the Word, but it is still "human obedience, an obedience, however, which is not a "work" but is "enabled" to be what it is by God's power and his Spirit."[20] Wagner considers Paul's faith as "man's response to God's initiative . . . an

---

13 "Bei Pls tritt πιστεύειν/π. Ganz in den Mittelpunkt seines „theol. Denkens. Er übernimmt dabei die allg.–chrislt. Bedeutung der Annahme der Botschaft von Gottes Heilshandeln in Christus." Barth, πίστις, col. 224–5. "Hat Gott ein für allemal im Kreuz Christi heilschaffend gehandelt, so kann die Antwort des Menschen nur in der gehorsamen Annahme im Sich-Verlassen auf Gottes χάρις, im Sich-beschenken-Lassen mit und im Leben aus dieser Gabe bestehen." Barth, πίστις, col., 225.

14. Barth, πίστις, col., 225.

15. Barth, πίστις, col., 226.

16. Wagner, "Interpretation."

17. Wagner, "Interpretation," 55.

18. Wagner, "Interpretation," 56.

19. Wagner, "Interpretation," 56.

20. Wagner, "Interpretation," 57.

accepting of God's gifts."[21] Wagner, therefore, seems to fall into that same camp of scholars who regard faith as a result of God's word and His gifts, while still remaining a human exercise.

Richard B. Hays came to prominence with the 1983 publication of his dissertation *The Faith of Jesus Christ: The Narrative Substructure of Galatians 3:1–4:11*. The second edition of that dissertation appeared in 2002 and included a challenging essay by James D. G. Dunn and a response by Hays. His work occasioned a re-opening of the interpretation of the Pauline phrase πίστις Χριστοῦ. Is it an objective genitive or a subjective? Hays chooses the latter, I contend, because his understanding of faith is that of a meritorious human work.

Hays places faith in the role of an "Object" that is "communicated to humanity through Christ's redemptive action."[22] "If this is correct," he continues, "Gal 3:22 must not be interpreted to mean that believers receive the promise by the subjective act of placing their faith in Jesus Christ; instead, it must mean that Jesus Christ, by the power of faith, has performed an act which allows believers to receive the promise." By labeling faith a "subjective act" Hays must mean that he understands faith as human achievement. At the same time, however, he labels faith as a power that enables Christ to complete his ministry. This is in accord with his earlier understanding of faith as assuming the "actantial role of Helper" and that Christ's mission was "achieved through the aid of πίστις."[23] It therefore seems that Hays views faith as a human act but when speaking of Christ's faith, it is a power. It seems we are dealing with two different perspectives on faith, one human; one divine. We will continue with human faith.

Hays quotes William Law: "Suppose one man to rely on his own faith and another to rely on his own works, then faith of the one and the works of the other are equally the same filthy rags."[24] On the next page Hays writes that a popular understanding of faith "has always carried with it the risk of turning faith into another kind of work, a human achievement." Hays seems to agree with this interpretation when on the same page he speaks of faith as a "psychological disposition" and "intellectual assent." He acknowledges that some scholars have not understood faith as a work but rather as a gift. He questions, however, whether this "sort of explanation may be read

21. Wagner, "Interpretation," 58.
22. Hays, *Faith of Jesus Christ*, 116.
23. Hays, *Faith of Jesus Christ*, 105.
24. Hays, *Faith of Jesus Christ*, 119.

into our texts in Galatians."[25] Further on Hays describes faith as an "act of believing/trusting"[26] and "the individual activity of "believing.""[27]

Hays asserts that those who accept the traditional rendering of ἐξ ἀκοῆς πίστεως in Gal 3:2 and 5 do so on the understanding that Paul is contrasting the hearing of faith with yet another human activity: works of law.[28] He continues this line of thought on p. 130 where he remarks on Gal 3:2–5 and the "hearing of faith": "In the second place, the whole passage makes better sense if we suppose that Paul's primary intention is not at all to juxtapose one type of human activity ('works') to another ('believing/hearing') but rather to juxtapose human activity to God's activity, as revealed in the 'proclamation.'"

It appears that Hays regards faith as human activity or "works" and therefore wishes to translate πίστις Χριστοῦ in a new fashion in order to avoid what he would identify as a misinterpreted juxtaposition of similar concepts.

On p. 131 Hays describes the gospel as "the message that evokes faith." Evokes is a term he has chosen deliberately. This term, according to the Oxford American Dictionary and Language Guide (1999) defines the term evoke to mean: "1. inspire or draw forth (memories, feelings, a response, etc.). 2. summon (a supposed spirit from the dead) . . . [*L evocare*] as E–, *vocare* call)]"—"To summon or call forth: *actions that evoked our mistrust.*'" Does Hays think that faith is inspiration that comes from outside a person or something that exists in everyone and is drawn out of the person? The answer comes on p. 132 where he writes that Paul emphasized not the "individual act of believing" but rather the "proclaimed message (ἀκοή), which calls forth faith, as the means by which the Spirit is given." Now we see that Hays indeed regards the term evoke as meaning to draw out or to call forth, not to inspire. Inspiration involves the introduction of something from outside the person, not calling forth something that was already there.

Though Hays admits that faith can mean a "life-giving power external to the individual," in that very same sentence he says that for Paul it is "a phenomenon within the consciousness of the individual subject."[29] Which is it, or does one follow from the other? But Hays drops the other shoe

25. Hays, *Faith of Jesus Christ*, 122.

26. Hays, *Faith of Jesus Christ*, 123.

27. Hays, *Faith of Jesus Christ*, 124.

28. Hays, *Faith of Jesus Christ*, 126.

29. Hays, *Faith of Jesus Christ*, 154.

when on p. 211 he writes, "because justification hinges upon this action of Jesus Christ, upon an event *extra nos*, it is a terrible and ironic blunder to read Paul as though his gospel made redemption contingent upon our act of deciding to dispose ourselves toward God in a particular way." This is as unequivocal a statement about the origin and nature of faith that we are likely to find in Hays's book. Faith for Richard Hays is a human act of decision. He repeats this same sentiment on p. 293 where he describes faith as "our own cognitive disposition or confessional orthodoxy." Faith, for Hays, is a work of human achievement. Perhaps, like Mundle, Hays is confused because the Apostle's language can be confusing.

Following a course set by Schweitzer, though Hays does not consider it an "exhaustive explanation,"[30] he advocates for a kind of participatory soteriology when he writes, "'faith' is not the precondition for receiving God's blessing; instead it is the appropriate mode of response to a blessing already given in Christ. As such, it is also the mode of participation in the pattern definitively enacted in Jesus Christ: as we respond in faith, we participate in an ongoing reenactment of Christ faithfulness."[31] Further on he writes, "The relation between our faith and the faith of Christ is similarly metaphorical: our faith answers and reflects his—indeed, *participates in* his—because according to Paul it is God's design for us 'to be conformed to the image of his Son' (Rom 8:20)."[32] Faith, for Hays, is a human response to what Christ has done and is somehow the means whereby the human being participates in Christ's faithfulness.

This participatory soteriology is, Hays explains, like identifying with a character in a story![33] Is that how people are saved in Paul's theology? Are they redeemed by identifying with Jesus of Nazareth in the same way as perhaps, they might have identified with Odysseus in Homer or Aeneas in Virgil? Hays allows that this "story-participation" does not exhaust every means by which people participate in Christ. They also participate in Christ through the sacraments, spiritual experience, and the Church. But it

30. Hays, *Faith of Jesus Christ*, 215.

31. Hays, *Faith of Jesus Christ*, 211.

32. Hays, *Faith of Jesus Christ*, 297. Hays translates Gal 2:20 to read: "I participate in the pattern of faith enacted by the Son of God, who loved me and gave himself up for me." Hays, *Faith of Jesus Christ*, 212.

33. "If Paul's gospel is the story of Jesus Christ, then we might participate in Christ in somewhat the same way that we participate in (or identify with) the protagonist of any story." Such identification is a "spontaneous response elicited by the story." Hays, *Faith of Jesus Christ*, 214.

is "participation in the gospel story" that constitutes the common grounding of all such participation.[34]

In the introduction to the second edition of his dissertation he re-emphasizes the theme of "participatory soteriology," considering it the "key" to St. Paul's soteriology.[35] "*In a mysterious way, Jesus has enacted our destiny, and those who are in Christ are shaped by the pattern of his self-giving death. He is the prototype of redeemed humanity.*"[36] This soteriology is, according to Hays, the remedy for Gerhard Ebeling's complaint that post-Reformation theology could not account for a link between justification and Christology. "The greatest strength of the exegesis set forward in *Faith of Jesus Christ* . . . is that it explains how Paul's understanding of the πίστις of Jesus is integrally related to his understanding of δικαιοσύνη."[37] Does it explain that? If Jesus of Nazareth was a believer and died in that faith, then good for him! But what does that have to do with us? How are we connected to that event and its importance in any meaningful way? How does Christ "embrace" me and how do I "share" in the significance of his life and death? Hays claims we are "taken up into his life, including his faithfulness, and that faithfulness therefore imparts to us the shape of our own existence."[38] He refers to Morna Hooker's "'interchange' soteriology" in which the faith of Christ ought to be understood as "a concentric expression, which begins, always, from the faith of Christ himself, but which includes, necessarily, the answering faith of believers, who claim that faith as their own."[39] He writes that "being united with Christ is salvific because to share his life is to share in the life of God."[40] Yet, nowhere does Hays tell us what this sharing, being taken up, participation, or claiming actually is. If it is like identifying with a character in a story, then it is mere role playing. I read a biography of Theodore Roosevelt when I was a young boy and marveled at the episode in which he shot a stag that died before it hit the ground. I may have wished to "identify" myself with Teddy at the time, but I shall never be able to make

34. Hays, *Faith of Jesus Christ*, 215.

35. Hays, *Faith of Jesus Christ*, xxix.

36. Hays, *Faith of Jesus Christ*, xxix, [Hays's italics.] Hays remarks on p. xlviii that my opposition to his thesis is unsettling "since it seems to suggest a view that Jesus was not human." It suggests nothing of the kind, only that Hays's view of faith is founded on his own unexamined presuppositions.

37. Hays, *Faith of Jesus Christ*, xxix.

38. Hays, *Faith of Jesus Christ*, xxxii.

39. Hays, *Faith of Jesus Christ*, xxxii.

40. Hays, *Faith of Jesus Christ*, xxxiii.

a shot like that! If one cannot fully identify with a human character, how is one to do so with divinity? Asylums are well populated by people who have identified themselves with Napoleon Bonaparte. Mere identification with another person as an answer to the issue is far from adequate.

On the other hand, Hays does approach a better solution when he cites Sam K. Williams's thought about Christ as the "creator of a new domain or 'power field.'"[41] Hays acknowledges that the proclamation of the gospel has power on p. 130, and that that power works miracles, but he never applies any such language to human faith. As we shall see later on, it is this aspect of power that gives faith profound significance for humanity.

It appears from these quotations that Richard Hays assumes faith to be a human achievement. Though he can at times describe it as a power outside of the human being, he nonetheless expresses himself most clearly on the matter when he describes faith as a human decision or cognitive disposition. Because he understands faith in such a fashion he wishes to re-translate πίστις Χριστοῦ as a subjective genitive in order, in his mind, to avoid what he considers to be an inappropriate juxtaposition between human faith and human works. This is a noble attempt to emphasize God's grace, but if, as will be argued below, faith is not a human work but rather a transformative gift of divine power, then the supposed need to avoid any opposition between two forms of human works is like chasing a phantom of one's own imagination.[42]

Hays's idea about participating in Christ through one's identification with Christ (as with a character in a story) and thus somehow sharing in Christ's faithfulness, lacks any meaningful or enduring connection between God and the human being. Many people identify with characters in novels or in history and such identification may change them in some way, but it cannot thereby procure their eternal salvation. Moreover, a faith that answers and reflects another's cannot be precisely the same faith because it has a different source. If faith, according to Hays, is merely a human work, but Christ's faith is, by definition, divine, then how can a finite being reflect, share, or somehow participate in something that is decidedly "other" and foreign to the self? What actual connection is there other than one's human imagination and is that enough for salvation? Whatever he might mean by

41. Hays, *Faith of Jesus Christ*, xxxi. See also p. 279 where he writes, "The phrase 'from faith for faith' then becomes a rhetorically effective slogan to summarize the gospel message of a salvation that originates in God's power and is received trustingly by the beneficiaries of that power."

42. See Silva, "Faith Versus Works," 234.

"participate," it is evident that such participation is human imagination, not divine redemption. It is therefore to be classified with the "filthy rags" of human faith and thus no more effective in salvation than any other human "work."

The solution that Hays provides is based, in my opinion, on a mistaken reading of faith in St. Paul's theology and constitutes no better solution to the problem of salvation than the traditional readings Hays disparages and the mistaken reading he adopts. He exhibits the same problem as that contained in Schweitzer's work: he is unwilling to entertain the possibility that faith is a gift.

Morna D. Hooker displays a more ambivalent view of the genesis of faith in her article entitled ΠΙΣΤΙΣ ΧΡΙΣΤΟΥ.[43] Hooker regards faith as "the believer's response" or "human response to God's action in Christ."[44] She says that πίστις Χριστοῦ should be considered a "concentric expression, which begins, always, from the faith of Christ himself, but which includes, necessarily, the answering faith of believers, who claim that faith as their own."[45] From such comments it would appear that Hooker regards faith as a human work. However, Hooker clearly denies this when she writes, "Faith is certainly not to be understood as a form of human works! Faith derives, *not* from the believer, but from the fact that he or she is already in Christ and identified with him."[46] The question then arises as to how one enters into Christ or identifies with Christ.

For an answer Hooker suggests a "pattern of interchange between Christ and the believer."[47] But an explanation of the precise means by which any interchange takes place is elusive. Is the ritual of baptism the means by which one becomes "in" Christ as Hooker briefly mentions?[48] Or, does one come into Christ through faith as Hooker seems to suggest on p. 340 where she writes, "It is the faith/faithfulness of Christ which lead to the Cross; and it is by their faith that believers share his death and risen life." Thus, Hooker says, contradictorily, that one's faith derives from one's already being in

---

43. Hooker, "ΠΙΣΤΙΣ ΧΡΙΣΤΟΥ," 321–42.

44. Hooker, "ΠΙΣΤΙΣ ΧΡΙΣΤΟΥ," 322.

45. Hooker, "ΠΙΣΤΙΣ ΧΡΙΣΤΟΥ," 341.

46. Hooker, "ΠΙΣΤΙΣ ΧΡΙΣΤΟΥ," 341.

47. Hooker, "ΠΙΣΤΙΣ ΧΡΙΣΤΟΥ," 332.

48. When commenting on 2 Cor 1:17–22 Hooker asks about the process by which one comes into Christ. "Paul is clearly thinking of baptism into Christ, and also of participation in Christ." Hooker, "ΠΙΣΤΙΣ ΧΡΙΣΤΟΥ," 334.

Christ (as quoted above), but, at the same time, one's being in Christ is effected through one's faith. The reader is left to ponder the paradox.

Notwithstanding this dilemma, it is clear that one of the reasons Hooker approves of Richard Hays's interpretation is that it would place greater emphasis on Christ's action, not ours. "But to take πίστις Χριστοῦ as a reference to Christ's own faith/faithfulness is in fact in no way to neglect the faith of the believer; and to take it of the believer's faith in Christ may emphasize that faith at the expense of stating what *Christ* has done."[49] At the end of her article Hooker says that to render πίστις Χριστοῦ as a subjective genitive would result in stressing the role of Christ in the believer's life.[50]

Hooker writes that faith is not a work but that people must answer the faith of Christ and claim that faith as their own. In other words, faith is not a human work, yet humans have to do it. She offers a kind of "interchange" between Christ and the believer, which is prior to faith, but leaves the means of that interchange open to question. She laudably, as with Hays, wishes to emphasize Christ's work in salvation rather than human faith but leaves the reader perplexed as to the nature of the connection between the devotee and the object of devotion.[51]

J. Louis Martyn shares the common confusion of faith as a human deed but not a work in his commentary on Galatians in the Anchor Bible Series.[52] Martyn says that faith is "elicited, kindled, incited by the faith of Christ, enacted in his atoning death."[53] He uses such language frequently to describe the genesis of human faith.[54] At first glance, Martyn seems to suggest that faith is a fruit of the Holy Spirit when he remarks that "faith is

49. Hooker, "ΠΙΣΤΙΣ ΧΡΙΣΤΟΥ," 322.

50. Hooker, "ΠΙΣΤΙΣ ΧΡΙΣΤΟΥ," 342.

51. Dr. Hooker recently penned a further article, "Another look at πίστις Χρισοῦ," 46–62, in which she argues that the phrase refers mainly to Christ's faith but also can refer to human faith as well. She concludes "that this faith is possible only because it is a sharing in his" [Christ's]. She does not elaborate any further from her earlier article as to just how such "sharing" is accomplished. She also mistakenly regards Mark W. Elliott's article ("Πίστις Χριστοῦ," 277–89) as arguing the opposite of my article, "ΠΙΣΤΙΣ ΧΡΙΣΤΟΥ," 233–41. On the contrary, Elliott's article is rather affirming of my work, concluding on p. 289, "In any case, any 'reintroduction' of 'the faith of Jesus Christ' will occur, it seems, *despite* the evidence of the witness of the tradition of Christian theology."

52. Martyn, *Galatians*.

53. Martyn, *Galatians*, 314.

54. See Martyn, *Galatians*, 146, 271–72, 289, 297, 299, 312, 314, 322, 333, 361–62, 375, 472, and 474.

more than a onetime occurrence. Like gentle humility, faith is a mark of the fruit that the Spirit is bearing in the daily life of the community of Christ."[55] However, it becomes clear on p. 289 that he does not consider the genesis of faith to be a divine action, but rather human when he says in footnote 22 that Bonnard is going too far when he suggests that preaching produces faith. Martyn insists that this goes too far in avoiding speaking of faith "as a human deed." In fact, Martyn regularly speaks of the "act" of faith on the part of human beings.[56]

Martyn says that though faith is a human deed it is not an autonomous human act or decision. "On the contrary, for Paul faith does not lie in the realm of human possibility."[57] Rather than speaking of faith as a deed reflecting the freedom of human will it is rather a deed that reflects "God's freeing of the will."[58] From this we may understand that faith issues from the freed human will, but from the human will nevertheless. Therefore, the question is whether, according to Martyn, faith is a gift or something engendered by the human being, although provoked by divine activity. It would seem safe to assume that for Martyn faith is a human deed, however it may be incited.

N. T. Wright is one of the most influential Christian theologians today and has written extensively on the New Testament and the letters of St. Paul. His view of faith is nuanced and includes elements of human ability and divine grace, together with the working of the Holy Spirit. His description of the genesis of faith is confusing because of the manner in which he describes the variegated nature of faith in St. Paul's epistles.

Wright understands faith in St. Paul's letters primarily as the human response to God's divine action. In *Paul in Fresh Perspective* Wright refers to "human faith" or "human belief or trust in the Messiah."[59] This view is carried over to his *Justification: God's Plan & Paul's Vision* and in his *Paul and the Faithfulness of God*.

In *Justification* Wright describes faith as human appropriation of what God has done.[60] He designates faith as a response when he writes, "the proper response to a promise—particularly a promise from God!—is

---

55. Martyn, *Galatians,* 499.

56. See Martyn, *Galatians,* 252, 297, and 314.

57. Martyn, *Galatians,* 276.

58. Martyn, *Galatians,* 276.

59. Wright, *Paul in Fresh Perspective,* 112, 120.

60. Wright, *Justification,* 204.

to believe it."[61] Wright contends that for Paul faith is what God requires from people and that the kind of faith exhibited by Abraham constitutes the mark of true humanity.[62]

Wright asks how such faith comes to be; the very question this study addresses. He is concerned that faith is not understood as a kind of "work" and therefore uses the language of evoking faith as a way to skirt such misunderstanding. "God evokes this faith in people from Abraham to the present day and beyond."[63] When considering Galatians 3:2 and 5 and the phrase "hearing of faith," Wright concludes that the proper understanding of the phrase is "the message that elicited faith."[64] Thus, he uses the same language as that of Richard Hays who also writes of faith that is elicited. Does this mean that Wright thinks faith is something that is drawn out of the person, called forth from the individual, and therefore a capacity that existed prior to God's eliciting or evoking?

On the other hand, (and on the same page) Wright also uses the language of transformation when he writes of Paul's understanding of God's call, "What he refers to as God's 'call' (Rom 8:28 and frequently) is the moment when, out of sheer grace, the word of the gospel, blown on by the powerful wind of the Spirit, transforms hearts and minds so that, although it is known to be ridiculous and even shameful, people come to believe that Jesus is Lord."[65] Is this transforming the same as eliciting and evoking faith? When Wright uses the language of transformation is he equating that with the language of eliciting?

He rightly emphasizes the work of the Holy Spirit in all of this but at the same time assumes that human faith and the working of the Holy Spirit are two different things. "You cannot, in short, have a Pauline doctrine of assurance . . . without the Pauline doctrine of the Spirit. Try to do it, and you will put too much weight on human faith, which will then generate all kinds of further questions about types of faith, about faith and feelings,

---

61. Wright, *Justification*, 208.

62. "Faith of Abraham's kind is the sign of a genuine humanity, responding out of total human weakness and helplessness to the grace and power of God, and thus giving God the glory." Abraham's faith for Paul, according to Wright, "indicates the presence of genuine, humble, trusting, and indeed we might say image-bearing humanity. . . . And, within that, "faithfulness" has all along (so it seems) been the thing that God requires from his people." Wright, *Justification*, 209.

63. Wright, *Justification*, 210.

64. Wright, *Justification*, 210.

65. Wright, *Justification*, 210.

about what happens when faith wobbles."[66] The Pauline doctrine of the Spirit, according to Wright, is separate from human faith. It seems that one must emphasize the one or the other because Wright, as others before him, has drawn a line between the two. Yet, if there is a line of demarcation between Spirit and faith, how is it that the Spirit transforms hearts and minds? Would not the latter thought explode the barrier between faith and Spirit?

In *Paul and the Faithfulness of God*, Wright continues his use of the language of faith as human response and of evoking faith.[67] However, he is somewhat reluctant to describe the actual production of faith: "when the gospel is announced, the spirit works through the message that is proclaimed. The result, one way or another, is 'faith.'"[68]

He describes faith as a "badge" that marks out the believer and which includes both the concept of faith as trust and faithfulness.[69] As in *Justification* he writes about faith being evoked but he also describes it as being produced by the Holy Spirit.[70]

Paradox best describes the understanding of Paul's faith in the writings of N. T. Wright. In *Justification* he expresses this paradox clearly when he writes, "And it is by the energy of the Spirit, working in those who belong to the Messiah, that the new paradox comes about in which the Christian really does exercise free moral will and effort but at the same time ascribes this free activity to the Spirit."[71] On the next page he asserts that "with this paradox (the Spirit works within us, we freely work) comes a careful balance."[72]

---

66. Wright, *Justification*, 237.

67. Wright, *Paul and the Faithfulness*, 839, 920.

68. Wright, *Paul and the Faithfulness*, 920.

69. "Those who believe the gospel, 'who believe in the one who raised from the dead Jesus our lord' (4.24), are thus appropriately marked out by that badge of pistis, their own pistis, not as an arbitrary sign, not because it means that they have had some kind of religious experience and so must have been converted, not because 'faith' is a special, meritorious form of interiority which this God decides to reward, but because pistis, faithfulness, (a) always was supposed to be the badge of Israel, (b) now has been the badge of Jesus, and so (c) is the appropriate badge—the only badge!—by which Jesus' followers are to be marked out." Wright, *Paul and the Faithfulness*, 839–40.

70. "As for the pistis upon which this status of dikaiosyne is declared, we should assume that here as elsewhere in Paul it is the work of the spirit through the gospel. . . . That spirit-led worship, as in Galatians 4.7, is part of what Paul means by pistis." Wright, *Paul and the Faithfulness*, 991.

71. Wright, *Justification*, 236.

72. Wright, *Justification*, 237.

Is it truly a paradox that on the one side we have human faith that is the effort of the person him or herself and that on the other side we have the working of the Holy Spirit to produce faith and transform the individual into a believer? Or is it merely a misunderstanding of faith on a basic level and a confusion of terms? As we have seen with other scholars, so we see it in Wright's works that there remains a bifocal nature to the theology of faith, with a barrier between divine action and human response that necessarily produces a paradoxical theological assertion that on the one hand humans must put forth some effort, but on the other hand, never take credit for it. This might make sense in the refined halls of academe but it will not escape the withering logic of any clever teenager who knows that if you place effort in anything, you are responsible for it, and therefore must be credited for it, not as a gift but as a right, as something owed. Whenever theologians try to split hairs in order to express a profound theological concept they must be aware that far from impressing their peers, it is the church at large that remains their true interlocutor. In that church are plain thinking people who recognize truth when they see it, as well as obfuscation. They also recognize the difference between paradox and contradiction; between profundity and confusion. Above all, in their hearts they know that when one puts out effort, be it physical or spiritual, it is something for which one is creditable. Even if that effort is slight and insignificant, even if it is a tiny percentage of the whole, still it is something for which human beings may boast not only before God but before all. A better means of describing the faith of St. Paul must be found if we are to release the church from confusion.

In 1978 Hans-Jürgen Hermisson and Eduard Lohse collaborated on a book on faith in the Old and New Testaments.[73] In the section dealing with Pauline faith the authors describe faith as a human answer to the Gospel.[74] Faith is described mostly as an acceptance.[75] However, the accepting or answering faith of humans cannot be construed as praiseworthy or meritorious under the law.[76] Hermisson and Lohse comment on the origin of faith

73. Hermisson and Lohse, *Faith*.

74. "The sinner's justification, acquired in baptism, is itself acquired by the answer of faith." Hermisson and Lohse. *Faith*, 145.

75. "It is preached in the gospel and accepted by faith." Hermisson and Lohse, *Faith*, 137. "Faith arises from the affirming acceptance of the Christian proclamation, an acceptance standing at the beginning of being a Christian." Hermisson and Lohse, *Faith*, 145. With this emphatic remark he underscores that only in faith can that proof of God's righteousness be comprehended and accepted." Hermisson and Lohse, *Faith*, 138.

76. "Anyone accepting this message relinquishes any self-praise or the possibility of

in a dual manner by writing that faith arises from the power of the word, but at the same time this faith is conscious that it is being addressed by that word.[77] Faith, it seems, is somehow impressed with that word and accepts it as true and worthy of its trust. But this faith is definitely human.[78] It is this faith that "acquires" justification.[79] Because they understand faith as an acceptance and answer to the Gospel they can also identify faith with obedience.[80]

Thus, Hermisson and Lohse seem to be caught in the same dilemma we have encountered previously. At one and the same time, faith has its origin in a divine power, but it is decidedly a human action, only without merit.

In 1983, a collection of ecumenical theologians met in Rome to discuss "The Apostolic Faith in the Scriptures and in the Early Church." They produced a volume edited by Hans-Georg Link entitled "The Roots of Our Common Faith," which contains a section by Günther Wagner on the faith of St. Paul.[81] In that section Wagner points out that St. Paul does not define faith, nor does he identify it as a virtue or an attitude.[82] Wagner, however, describes Paul's faith in a very familiar way as an "act," an "acceptance," and an "exercise."[83] Hearing the gospel "evokes" faith.[84] Faith has its origin in the word, but it is still "human obedience, an obedience, however, which is not a 'work' but is 'enabled' to be what it is by God's power and his Spirit."[85]

---

wanting to assert oneself with the help of the law, and from now on lives in faith in Christ." Hermisson and Lohse, *Faith,* 146. "Faith is free from any appearance of self-praise, and rather represents its complete opposite." Hermisson and Lohse, *Faith,* 142–43.

77. "Faith does not grow from seeing, and certainly not from some compelling proof, but only from the power of the word which faith knows is addressing it." Hermisson and Lohse. *Faith,* 141–42.

78. In commenting on the faith of Abraham in Paul's epistle the authors write that it is "a story that speaks in an exemplary fashion of divine righteousness and man's faith." Hermisson and Lohse, *Faith,* 138.

79. Hermisson and Lohse, *Faith,* 145.

80. Faith answering to the gospel can thus also be called obedience by Paul (Rom 1:5; 10:16; 19:19; and elsewhere), since an affirming posture necessarily results in the gospel itself determining the believer's life and action from then on." Hermisson and Lohse, *Faith,* 146.

81. Wagner, "Interpretation."

82. Wagner, "Interpretation," 55.

83. Wagner, "Interpretation," 56.

84. Wagner, "Interpretation," 56.

85. Wagner, "Interpretation," 57.

Wagner considers Paul's faith as "Man's response to God's initiative . . . an accepting of God's gifts."[86] Wagner, therefore, seems to fall into that same camp of scholars who regard faith as a result of God's word and His gifts, but still a very human result.

Stephen W. Need offered a reading of St. Paul's theology in which he tackled a number of issues, among them, faith.[87] He rejects the medieval reading of St. Paul that concerned itself with "good works and indulgences" and the Patristic and Reformation teachings of imputed righteousness.[88] Need clearly understands St. Paul's concept of faith as a human response to God's initiative.[89] Faith is the human part of a process in which God and humanity work together.[90] Faith is not an inevitable response, only a possible one.[91] Though faith has a divine dimension to it, Need seems to emphasize human freedom of response when it comes to faith.

In his rereading of the letter to the Romans, Stanley K. Stowers asserts that Paul's letter was written to Gentiles, the interpretation of which has been clouded by subsequent Christian readers' preoccupation with sin, guilt, and salvation.[92] He regards "faithfulness" as the best translation of *pistis* in St. Paul's letters.[93] He writes that the traditional view of faith has been

86. Wagner, "Interpretation," 58.

87. Need, *Paul Today*.

88. Need, *Paul Today*, 125–26.

89. "Those who respond in faith (*pistis*) or trust in God's initiative in Christ will enter into the new relationship. It is not a mechanical imputation that means human beings will automatically henceforth always do righteous acts. It is not that believers are automatically 'made' righteous, but that they have a new possibility before them to which they may or may not respond in faith. Their response in faith will then, as it were, activate the process of justification." Need, *Paul Today*, 133.

90. "However one understands the words, it seems that the real effectiveness of the process lies not just in God doing everything, even though he takes the initiative, but in God and humanity working together in the process. To be 'justified' is to accept the offer made by God in faith and to act accordingly." Need, *Paul Today*, 134. "Faith is the human side of the process." Need, *Paul Today*, 135.

91. "And in all this, faith is not the basis of justification and righteousness but a possible response to an offer made by God." Need, *Paul Today*, 135. "God works with humanity in the justification of his people, and they may or may not respond to him in faith. They are not simply 'made' righteous but are given the opportunity of participating in a new relationship established by God in Christ." Need, *Paul Today*, 136.

92. Stowers, *Rereading of Romans*.

93. "I have chosen 'faithfulness' as the most satisfactory translation for many texts, although I am often not entirely happy with any English word. Paul associates pistis with obedience to God, and "trusting obedience" is sometimes a possible translation.

to regard it as a "mental act" or "attitude" and that such a reading should be critiqued more thoroughly.[94] Though "faithfulness" provides the better English translation, Stowers writes that Paul associates *pistis* with obedience to God, and "trusting obedience" is sometimes a possible translation. At other times, the emphasis is on confidence in God's promises, and "trust" makes a good translation.[95]

When discussing the mention of the patriarch Abraham in St. Paul's epistles, Stowers remarks that "God did not require Abraham to keep a code of specific commandments as a prerequisite for accepting him. God's approach required Abraham's trust in the divine promises in a way that ensured Abraham's faithfulness to the hopes embodied in the promises."[96] That he understands this trust as a human capacity is clear when he writes about "Abraham's act of faithfulness."[97] It appears that Stowers understands God's righteousness as a divine response to such human "faithfulness."[98] People seem to share in this "faithfulness" by somehow "participating in Christ's life."[99] God may graciously bestow righteousness upon a person, but only after that person has properly exhibited *pistis* as faithfulness and demonstrated the appropriate obedience.

Jürgen Becker's comprehensive treatment of St. Paul's theology contains a chapter that, of course, includes the topic of faith.[100] In that section, Becker describes faith as "the desired human response to the Christian missionary message."[101] Faith is placing "oneself in an all-inclusive, lifelong

---

At other times, the emphasis lies on confidence in God's promises, and 'trust' makes a good translation. Used of God, as in 3:3, it means his faithfulness to his commitments and 'obligations.' Used of Abraham and Christ, it describes their confidence in God's promises." Stowers, *Rereading of Romans*, 199.

94. Stowers, *Rereading of Romans*, 199.

95. "Paul associates *pistis* with obedience to God, and 'trusting obedience' is sometimes a possible translation. At other times, the emphasis is on confidence in God's promises, and 'trust' makes a good translation." Stowers, *Rereading of Romans*, 199.

96. Stowers, *Rereading of Romans*, 228.

97. Stowers, *Rereading of Romans*, 230. Also, "This was Abraham's faithfulness: Not lawkeeping [sic] but acting as circumstances required in light of God's promises." Stowers, *Rereading of Romans*, 228.

98. "The law teaches that the ungodly cannot be made righteous by works of the law but only on the basis of God's grace in response to human faithfulness." Stowers, *Rereading of Romans*, 241.

99. Stowers, *Rereading of Romans*, 318.

100. Becker, *Paul*.

101. Becker, *Paul*, 512.

relationship with God."[102] But faith can also be lacking and weak: "This is all true because faith is an affair of the 'heart' (cf. Rom. 10:9–10), and the center of the person will not always hold on with the same intensity and strength (1 Thess. 3:13) to the truth of faith: that whoever believes will not be put to shame (Rom. 10:11)."[103] Faith is a reliance that involves the whole person.[104]

On the other hand, faith is a result of the power of the word and a fruit of the Spirit.[105] But it seems that the Spirit only persuades one to believe.[106] Becker, therefore, agrees with many others that though faith is somehow connected with the Spirit and the Word, it is still the responsibility of the human being.

Jouette Bassler has navigated the waters of Pauline theology, and included an insightful discussion on the subject of faith.[107] She contends that, in speaking of faith, St. Paul emphasized the elements of trust and assent.[108] "Central, though, to the importance of the concept for Paul . . . is the conviction . . . that *pistis* is the appropriate and saving response to the gospel."[109] I assume that she means human trust, assent, and response.

Bassler next describes the prevailing view of St. Paul's concept of faith, following Bultmann. Faith, in this view, is "the antithesis of achievement."[110] Though "it is a 'free deed of decision,' it is not an accomplishment."[111] But Bassler acknowledges the paradox evident in many scholars that though faith cannot be construed as a meritorious human work that deserves God's justification, still this faith "*seems* like an accomplishment."[112] She recognizes the trap that Bultmann fell into when he insisted that though faith was a human act, it could not be labelled a meritorious religious "work."

---

102. Becker, *Paul,* 512.

103. Becker, *Paul,* 414.

104. Becker, *Paul,* 413.

105. Becker, *Paul,* 413.

106. "For Paul, no doubt, priority is given to the view that the Spirit is the present Christ in the gospel, which therefore has the power to persuade to faith (Rom. 1:16; 1 Cor. 15:45; 1 Cor. 3:17; Gal. 4:6)." Becker, *Paul,* 415.

107. Bassler, *Navigating Paul.*

108. Bassler, *Navigating Paul,* 23.

109. Bassler, *Navigating Paul,* 24.

110. Bassler, *Navigating Paul,* 26.

111. Bassler, *Navigating Paul,* 26.

112. Bassler, *Navigating Paul,* 26.

Yet, this faith was, according to Bultmann, the necessary precondition to receiving God's righteousness. Bassler rightly notes that Bultmann's scheme merely places faith in the place of meritorious works and makes faith seem like a work.[113]

Bassler contends that the prevailing view has misconstrued the Pauline opposition of faith and works and for this reason has misunderstood the nature of faith. She follows James D. G. Dunn in thinking that St. Paul does not oppose faith to works-righteousness, but rather to covenantal boundary markers and "Jewish national self-confidence based on their being the people of the law."[114] The Pauline phrase "works-righteousness" was merely meant to be ethnically inclusive.

Bassler, next, summarizes the πίστις Χριστοῦ issue. She thinks the subjective genitive option needs more exploration. "In particular, the relationship between Christ's faith and human faith needs to be explained."[115] She outlines three basic ways in which scholars have attempted to describe that relationship.[116] The first involves imitating Christ's example, the second involves identifying with Christ, and the third involves a mystical union or participation in Christ. She is interested, however, in "how one comes to be in Christ and the transformational implications of that union."[117] She finds direction in Morna Hooker's treatment of the issue and argues that human faith comes before union with Christ.[118] Bassler emphasizes the preposition εἰς in the Pauline phrase πίστις εἰς Χριστὸν, which she contends denotes "transfer terminology" and quotes Hooker: "One *believes* into Christ."[119]

> What this strange-sounding assertion seems to imply is that one moves into union with Christ through an act of Christlike trust. This act is not, however, mere imitation of Christ's *pistis*; it is an act that claims and receives Christ's saving *pistis* as one's own. On this model Christ's *pistis* and human *pistis*, though initially separate, fuse into one.[120]

113. Bassler, *Navigating Paul*, 26.

114. Bassler, *Navigating Paul*, 27, (quoting Dunn).

115. Bassler, *Navigating Paul*, 30.

116. Bassler, *Navigating Paul*, 30–31.

117. Bassler, *Navigating Paul*, 31.

118. Bassler, *Navigating Paul*, 31, quoting Hooker: "We cannot share in what Christ *is* until we enter him, and . . . we enter him by believing in him, so that our faith must come first."

119. Bassler, *Navigating Paul*, 31.

120. Bassler, *Navigating Paul*, 31.

Though Bassler refuses to take sides she does seem to accept the common view that faith, though it later may "fuse" with that of Christ, is still a human faith, at least initially. She does, however, point in an interesting direction when she argues that the subjective genitive rendering of πίστις Χριστοῦ leads to a coordination of two lines of Pauline thought that had once seemed contradictory: justification by faith on the one hand, and baptism into Christ on the other. "If faith involves participation in Christ, the two lines of thought merge into one."[121] There is another way to merge these two lines of thought that we will pursue later. Be that as it may, it seems that whatever the connection it has with Christ, Bassler considers faith a response of the individual.[122]

James D. G. Dunn's *The Theology of the Apostle Paul* contains a section on justification by faith, with familiar themes.[123] Dunn regards the faith of St. Paul as primarily "human believing."[124] This believing he characterizes as "utter dependence" and "unconditional trust."[125] It is a faith that was exercised by Abraham but not by Adam.[126] Abraham's faith was a response to the promises of God.[127] This holds true for all people.[128] This response is not merely a momentary event but continues through the Christian's life resulting in ethical obedience.[129]

Such faith, however, was not turned into a "work" by the Apostle.[130] But it does result in works of love to such an extent that faith and love,

---

121. Bassler, *Navigating Paul*, 32.

122. "This focused discussion of the importance of faith for the individual who responds—or does not—to the message of asalvation." Bassler, *Navigating Paul*, 32.

123. Dunn, *Theology of Paul*.

124. Dunn, *Theology of Paul*, 379, 381, 382, 384.

125. Dunn, *Theology of Paul*, 379.

126. Dunn, *Theology of Paul*, 379.

127. "Before that God, the only response could be faith, simple trust." Dunn, *Theology of Paul*, 378. "This was the faith of the creature wholly reliant upon and confident in God's promise because it was God who promised (4.21)." Dunn, *Theology of Paul*, 379.

128. "For Paul faith is the human response to all divine grace." Dunn, *Theology of Paul*, 634.

129. See his section on Faith and "the law of faith." Dunn, *Theology of Paul*, 634–42. "What is in view once again is not just a once and for all act of believing, but an ongoing relationship which embraces the whole of living, where faith is the 'port' through which the power of life flows." Dunn, *Theology of Paul*, 636.

130. Dunn, *Theology of Paul*, 638.

according to Dunn, should not be separated. Rather, as Gal 5:6 attests, faith "comes to expression in love."[131]

Thomas C. Oden's *The Justification Reader* exhibits a now familiar paradoxical description of Christian faith.[132] Before addressing faith, however, Oden comments on the concept of grace, remarking that the doctrine of salvation by grace was well established in the ancient church before the Reformation.[133] However, he quotes Cyril of Jerusalem: "It is God's part to confer grace, but yours to accept and guard it."[134] Oden then remarks, "While justification is imputed, wholly as a gift, another step is required: for *what is imputed seeks to be imparted*, given in such a way that spiritual gifts can be appropriated as acts of freedom."[135]

Oden maintains the same paradoxical description of faith as he does with grace. This is why Oden can say that though faith is a divine gift, it is still "a free human act."[136] "God does not believe for us, but enables our believing."[137] Oden insists that faith is "truly our own action" but one that is enabled by God's grace.[138] He regards faith as both activity and receptivity.[139] "While justification is imputed wholly as a gift, the gift itself seeks an active response."[140] Oden posits that God prepares human hearts for receiving grace and that when we do "it is God's own act enabling our act."[141] It seems that such a "dynamic" preserves free will in the person.[142]

Having taken such a general view of grace and faith, Oden defines faith as "the means by which salvation is appropriated through personal

131. Dunn, *Theology of Paul,* 638. "In short, faith in God (in and through Christ) was for Paul as much the basis for and means to right living as it was for and to being 'righteoused' (justified)." Dunn, *Theology of Paul,* 642.

132. Oden, *Justification Reader.*

133. Oden, *Justification Reader,* 106.

134. Oden, *Justification Reader,* 117.

135. Oden, *Justification Reader,* 117. Oden's italics.

136. Oden, *Justification Reader,* 117.

137. Oden, *Justification Reader,* 117.

138. Oden, *Justification Reader,* 118.

139. See his section 3. "Receptive Faith and Its Activity; Active Faith and Its Receptivity," in Oden, *Justification Reader,* 118–19.

140. Oden, *Justification Reader,* 119.

141. Oden, *Justification Reader,* 120.

142. Oden quotes St. Augustine's comments on Phil 2:12, 13 in his *On Grace and Free Will:* "It is certain that when we do a deed, the deed is ours; but he is the one who makes us do the deed." Oden, *Justification Reader,* 118. See also 123.

trust in the Son as Savior."[143] Citing Rom 3:1—4:25 he writes that the benefits of Christ's work are "applied by the Spirit and appropriated by the believer *through faith*."[144] This faith, however, is to be understood only as "the reception of grace," not as that which by itself saves people. As Philipp Melancthon stated, "The faithful are justified by grace, not by their own faith."[145]

Faith, for Oden, is the condition or means "by which the person appropriates Christ and his righteousness (Rom 1:17; 3:25; 4:20–22; Phil 3:8–11; Gal 2:16)."[146] Oden characterizes faith as a "decision" on the same page.[147]

In the end Oden argues for the capacity for faith within every human being:

> The faculty for faith, the possibility of trusting God, is primitively present in every human spirit, everybody in-breathed to life by God. Despite the recalcitrance of sin, this faculty is gradually, through revelation, in God's own time, being awakened by God's own Spirit, always looking toward his decisive coming in Christ. Meanwhile, the capacity for faith may to some extent lie dormant.[148]

Faith, therefore, for Oden is something enabled by God's grace as a gift, but it is something natural to every human person from birth and needs to be properly awakened so that it directs itself toward the proper object: Jesus Christ. This is why Oden, and others, I suspect, find it necessary to speak in paradoxical terms when attempting to deny any merit to faith in Christ while at the same time insisting that it is always a pre-existing capacity to be awakened or encouraged, etc. The difficulty is that whether one is given grace at the beginning of the process, at the middle, or at the end, it is still the human being who must be held accountable at some point and in some measure either for allowing faith to develop, making the right choice, or

---

143. Oden, *Justification Reader*, 129.

144. Oden, *Justification Reader*, 129.

145. Oden, *Justification Reader*, 137.

146. Oden, *Justification Reader*, 138.

147. "Faith freely resolves a life of righteousness grounded in the free gift of God's righteousness in Christ. This decision involves a renunciation of the devil and his powers, and all forms of idolatry."

148. Oden, *Justification Reader*, 150. On the same page he writes that "personal trust is providentially encouraged by common grace" and that grace "draws the person toward that saving faith."

recognizing the wonderful invitation to divine glory. If faith is an act of the human being that is not coerced or forced by God, then it is indeed grounds for boasting, even if in infinitesimal measure.

Stephen Westerholm has written a great deal on Pauline theology and is no defender of the New Perspective. Yet, he is also caught in the same dilemma or paradox of defining faith as a gift and a human response. In *Preface to the Study of Paul*, Westerholm several times designates faith as a response that is elicited, evoked, or awakened.[149] But this response, according to Westerholm, is not construed by the Apostle Paul as an "achievement."[150] God makes the first gracious move. Those who receive God's favor as a gift "are thereby moved to respond with faith: with trust, that is, in God's initiative of grace and goodness."[151] Westerholm maintains that rebellious humans cannot exhibit "behavior pleasing to God. They must first abandon their rebellion and submit to God in faith. This transformation of 'ungodly' people was not brought about by a unilateral decision on the part of the 'ungodly,' but through the proclamation of God's salvation."[152] In fact, "Adamic human beings, for Paul, cannot become God's people, or even respond to God's goodness in faith, unless God, acting on his own initiative, creates those possibilities; hence the need for the 'election' of believers."[153]

Westerholm continues in the same vein in *Perspectives Old and New on Paul: The "Lutheran" Paul and His Critics* in which he repeats the language of faith as response but not an "achievement."[154] Works of any kind that

---

149. "But the trust of mature human beings . . . is not a unilateral decision indifferent to the character of its object, but a response elicited by a perception of the trustworthiness or goodness of the one trusted." Westerholm, *Preface to the Study of Paul*, 52. "The natural, appropriate response evoked by the proclamation of the Christian message should thus be faith, or trust, in God: faith is awakened by hearing the word of Christ." Westerholm, *Preface to the Study of Paul*, 54. "Similarly, for Paul, a proper trust in God is awakened with the belief that he has acted on our behalf in Christ. . . . Their faith in God is itself not a product of their own initiative, but a response evoked by the news of God's staggering demonstration of goodness." Westerholm, *Preface to the Study of Paul*, 56.

150. "Although faith in the God who has demonstrated his love for humans in Christ is an inevitable requirement of the gospel, it is not, for Paul, an achievement of the believer." Westerholm, *Preface to the Study of Paul*, 55.

151. Westerholm, *Preface to the Study of Paul*, 106.

152. Westerholm, *Preface to the Study of Paul*, 56–57.

153. Westerholm, *Preface to the Study of Paul*, 112.

154. "Faith, in other words, is here a trusting response to a divine initiative that, because it trusts God to fulfill his word, abandons further efforts ('doing') at achieving the

demand recompense, and faith are not to be confused because the believer "benefits by divine grace without any consideration of personal merit."[155] "Justification is thus a gift of grace, received through faith, not gained by works."[156] Commenting on Philippians, Westerholm maintains that believers are granted "the privilege to believe in Christ (1:29) as preached by Paul in the gospel (cf. 1:5, 7, 12; 2:22; 4:3, 15)."[157] In fact, anything that believers do "remains a product of divine grace."[158] Yet, on the same page he makes the assertion that salvation is a future hope "to be attained by those who maintain their initial faith throughout their lives."[159] Paul may therefore charge the Philippians with working out their own salvation (Phil 2:12). But this maintenance is due to God who works in and through the believers.[160]

In *Understanding Paul*, Westerholm again returns to the theme of faith as a human response that does not jeopardize the Pauline concept of salvation by grace.[161] Yet, Westerholm still describes faith as something that is elicited or awakened within the individual.[162] He can also describe faith as something that been moved into existence: "What God has done for us through Christ should move us to trust him: faith is, for Paul, the appropriate human response to the gospel."[163]

---

same ends . . . a faith that credits and accepts what God offers." Westerholm, *Perspectives*, 311. "Such righteousness is contrasted with the righteousness 'from God that depends on faith': a *received* righteousness (cf. Rom 5:17), in other words, where one's own works are not a factor." Westerholm, *Perspectives*, 312.

155. Westerholm, *Perspectives*, 315.

156. Westerholm, *Perspectives*, 400.

157. Westerholm, *Perspectives*, 401.

158. Westerholm, *Perspectives*, 402n143.

159. Westerholm, *Perspectives*, 402.

160. "As they do, however, they need to recognize that God himself, working in and through them, brings about whatever they do (2:13)." Westerholm, *Perspectives*, 402.

161. "The required human response is that of 'faith.' . . . For the moment we need only note that the required response does nothing, in Paul's mind, to jeopardize the nature of divine redemption as a gift granted freely to sinners by the grace of God." Westerholm, *Understanding Paul*, 75.

162. "In requiring an object, then, trust is like love: it, too, is elicited, experienced, and expressed in ways dependent upon its object." Westerholm, *Understanding Paul*, 79. "But true trust, like (Barb and Bob's) love, does not come about through a simple decision made by the one who trusts. True trust is a response elicited by the trustworthiness or goodness of the one trusted." Westerholm, *Understanding Paul*, 79–80. "Similarly, for Paul, the belief that God has acted on our behalf in Christ awakens a proper trust in God." Westerholm, *Understanding Paul*, 82.

163. Westerholm, *Understanding Paul*, 87.

Westerholm comes very close to a consistent description of faith as a gracious gift of God, but cannot seem to relinquish the language of personal responsibility when it comes to believing in Christ. Though he is clear that whatever the believer does in faith, that person does so because of God's movement within the believer's life, he still uses the language of human responsibility when he writes about faith being elicited or awakened from within the person.

Francis Watson has written on *Paul and the Hermeneutics of Faith* and has made an attempt to go beyond the New Perspective.[164] He clearly regards the faith of St. Paul as a human response that is evoked or elicited.[165] As such, faith is a human act that acknowledges what God has done.[166] But this responsive human act is in turn responded to by God with a declaration of righteousness.[167] It seems that God initiates an action to which human beings respond, but then, in turn, reacts to that response.

In *Paul, Judaism, and the Gentiles*, Watson's purpose is "not to show that the theology which the Reformation tradition finds in Paul springs from a particular sociological context, but to show that key points in this

164. Watson, *Paul and the Hermeneutics*. Watson, *Paul, Judaism and the Gentiles*.

165. "Whether they think in terms of 'faithfulness' or of 'faith,' the prophet and the apostle are at one in their assumption that *emunah* or *pistis* refers to the human response to the divine promise of definitive, eschatological saving action. The apostles' message is 'gospel,' in which human speech is the bearer of 'the power of God unto salvation' to those in whom it evokes the response of faith (cf. Rom.1.16)." Watson, *Paul and the Hermeneutics*, 161. "In a two-way movement from Christ's death and back to it again, God's saving act in Christ seeks to elicit the answering faith that acknowledges it as what it truly is. Faith, then, is 'faith of Jesus Christ' in the dual sense that Jesus Christ, the embodiment of God's saving action, is as such both the origin and the object of faith." Watson, *Paul and the Hermeneutics*, 76.

166. "'Faith' is foundational to the divine-human relationship because faith alone is the human act that corresponds to the prior divine communicative action and is intended in it." Watson, *Paul and the Hermeneutics*, 193. "The term 'faith' speaks of the human recognition and acknowledgement of God as 'the God of my salvation.' Elicited by the divine word of the gospel and prefigured in the written prophetic vision." Watson, *Paul and the Hermeneutics*, 162. "In the one case, the emphasis falls on the human acknowledgement of God's eschatological saving action; in the other, it is human action in obedience to the law's prescriptions that constitutes the scriptural path to life." Watson, *Paul and the Hermeneutics*, 163.

167. "As in the case of Abraham, there is a human individual who believes, and there is a divine reaction to that fact which takes the form of a 'reckoning' as righteous (cf. Rom 4.3, citing Gen 15.6). 'By faith for faith' indicates that the instrumental relationship between faith and righteousness entails a free and intentional divine responsive action." Watson, *Paul and the Hermeneutics*, 51.

theology are not there in Paul at all."[168] When mentioning faith in Paul's letters, he remarks that for Paul "faith is dependent on and generated by the kerygma. . . . Yet, the genesis of faith in the kerygma does not reduce faith to passivity or eliminate its volitional dimension."[169] Watson wishes to point out that "even if, in some passages, Paul does stress the idea of the miraculous divine gift, in others he stresses the human activity through which the gift is appropriated."[170] Pauline faith, therefore, according to Watson, involves both divine gift and earthly response. He asserts that "concurrent human and divine work are necessary to bring about salvation."[171] But, as in his other book, the human response to divine initiative is again responded to by God and the declaration of justification is actually "*consequent on faith*."[172] "In the faith/justification sequence, a human act is indeed followed by a divine one."[173] Yet, Watson acknowledges that though "faith precedes and conditions the giving of the Spirit just as it precedes and conditions the bestowal of righteousness," faith "is itself preceded by and comprehended within the overarching divine saving act that Paul calls 'the redemption that is in Christ Jesus' (3:24)."[174] Faith "itself is the creation of the divinely authorized 'word' or gospel, rather than an autonomous production of the human 'free will' (cf. Rom. 1:1–6; 10:14–17)."[175] On the other hand, Watson insists that faith is a human act.[176]

Watson follows E. P. Sanders in his observation that St. Paul found Judaism objectionable because it was not Christianity.[177] Watson's support

168. Watson, *Paul, Judaism, and the Gentiles*, 121.

169. Watson, *Paul, Judaism, and the Gentiles*, 122.

170. Watson, *Paul, Judaism, and the Gentiles*, 126.

171. Watson, *Paul, Judaism, and the Gentiles*, 148.

172. Watson, *Paul, Judaism, and the Gentiles*, 236.

173. Watson, *Paul, Judaism, and the Gentiles*, 238.

174. Watson, *Paul, Judaism, and the Gentiles*, 238.

175. Watson, *Paul, Judaism, and the Gentiles*, 238.

176. "As presented by Paul, the divine act of justification follows the human act of faith, but both the human and the divine acts are moments within the comprehensive divine saving action that Paul here calls 'redemption' (ἀπολύτρωσις). The emphasis on 'faith' indicates that for Paul the divine saving action would be incomplete if it failed to secure human participation, in the form of its own acknowledgment." Watson, *Paul, Judaism, and the Gentiles*, 244.

177. "It is therefore correct to say, as E. P. Sanders does, that Paul opposes Judaism not because of any inherent errors such as 'self-righteousness' or 'legalism,' but simply *because it is not Christianity*. The present discussion attempts to give a historical and sociological grounding for this viewpoint." Watson, *Paul, Judaism, and the Gentiles*, 126.

for this point of view consists in his insistence that the contrast between "faith" on the one hand, and "works" on the other, constitutes merely the difference between two different religions and communal lives. "The faith/ works antithesis is not an antithesis between faith and morality-in-general, but an antithesis between life as a Christian, with its distinctive beliefs and practices, and life as an observant Jew."[178] Watson is of the mind that Judaism and Christianity are not two opposing religions, merely separate:

> Christ is incompatible with circumcision not because "Christ" symbolizes an abstract theological principle (receiving salvation as a sheer gift) that is incompatible with the equally abstract principle underlying circumcision (earning salvation through moral achievement), but because Paul has concluded that the church is only the church when it is separated from the Jewish community.[179]

If Watson is correct, then Judaism and Christianity are merely two fraternities in the same neighborhood. Though they may possess distinctive characteristics, fundamentally they are quite similar. Watson wishes to deconstruct any true opposition between the two faiths and render any moral or theological discrimination between them inert. This is why he contends that the opposition between faith and works in Paul's letters is not an opposition between God's grace and man's striving, but between two religious alternatives. Watson can achieve this sociological judgment because he thinks Paul's contrast between faith and works is not a contrast between "receiving salvation as a free gift and earning it by one's own efforts, but as an attempt to demarcate two different modes of communal practice."[180] Paul, according to Watson, was no Lutheran who believed in *sola gratia*

---

178. Watson, *Paul, Judaism, and the Gentiles*, 123. "In passages such as Galatians 2:216, the terms 'faith (of Jesus Christ)' and 'works (of law)' are selected and opposed to one another in order to signify the church's distinct, independent existence." Watson, *Paul, Judaism, and the Gentiles*, 123–24. "When Paul opposes 'works of the law,' he has in mind the distinctive way of life of the Jewish people, insofar as this is defined by the law of Moses. He is speaking of 'Judaism' (Gal 1:13, 14) and of nothing else." Watson, *Paul, Judaism, and the Gentiles*, 124. "Similarly, it is incorrect to assume that submission to the law of Moses within the Jewish community represents the religious person's striving after moral achievement. 'Works' represents nothing other than a specific communal way of life, defined in terms of the sacred text that is held to determine its distinctive characteristics and to establish its rationale." Watson, *Paul, Judaism, and the Gentiles*, 125.

179. Watson, *Paul, Judaism, and the Gentiles*, 130.

180. Watson, *Paul, Judaism, and the Gentiles*, 346.

"for Paul too, the responsive human obedience evoked by divine grace is a necessary precondition of salvation."[181]

Therefore, according to Watson, the Apostle to the Gentiles understood that faith in Christ was a similar act of obedience, evoked by grace or not, as any following of the Torah. As a consequence, Judaism and Christianity, at least for St. Paul, were inherently similar. Christianity and Judaism "are incompatible not because one stresses grace and the other achievement, but because the law is not observed in the Pauline congregations and because, as a result, the primary orientation in the one community and Moses in the other makes the two communities simply incommensurable."[182] The two "faiths" are mere alternatives.

If that is so, then why did the Apostle Paul risk life and limb (see 2 Cor 11:23–27), argue fervently and insultingly against the so-called "Judaizers" in Galatia, and spend the remainder of his life in a feverish missionary campaign to proclaim a faith that spelled the trashing of his old life (Phil 3:7–9)? If Christianity for St. Paul was a mere alternative to Judaism, then why did he bother to preach from Damascus to Rome and plan to bring his message to the end of the world? If St. Paul did not consider his Christian faith as of ultimate significance but only a mere religious preference, then why not choose something far easier to explain than a executed Messiah? There must have been a transcendent reason that struck to the very core of the Apostle's being that impelled him to a life spent delivering and arguing a message that he knew was universally both foolish and scandalous. Mere religious preference would not have been enough.

Hung-Sik Choi has written on faith in Galatians and clearly understands that faith has "a subjective anthropological element."[183] He draws a distinction and contrast between "the Christian's act of faith" (he uses that phrase or "human faith" almost thirty times in his article) in Christ and Christ's faithfulness. The latter is an historical event, whereas the former is merely subjective.[184] Commenting on Gal 5 he writes,

> The traditional anthropocentric reading of πίστις in 5:5 is highly unlikely; it does not mean the Christian's faith in Christ as the

---

181. Watson, *Paul, Judaism, and the Gentiles*, 346.

182. Watson, *Paul, Judaism, and the Gentiles*, 346.

183. Hung-Sik, "ΠΙΣΤΙΣ in Galatians," 475.

184. " . . . it is unlikely that ἡ πίστις in Gal 3:23–26 refers both to 'the faith of Christian' [*sic*] and to 'the faith of Jesus Christ,' since πίστις describes a historical event, not the Christian's subjective act of believing. Hung-Sik, "ΠΙΣΤΙΣ in Galatians," 478.

subjective condition of attaining the hoped-for righteousness. Nor does it describe the Christian's life as a reenactment of the pattern of faithfulness grounded and revealed in Jesus Christ. Nor does it function as the subjective psychological cause (i.e., the Christian's confidence) that makes Paul and the Galatians wait with eager longing for "the hoped-for righteousness." Rather it refers to the faithfulness of Christ, which is the objective soteriological basis of justification.[185]

Though he intriguingly associates Christ's faithfulness with "eschatological and apocalyptic power," he rejects that possibility for human faith.[186] He also understands the Pauline contrasts between circumcision/uncircumcision and faith working through love "not as different ways of life or human action but as conflicting redemptive-historical powers."[187]

Hung-Sik fully embraces the notion of human faith as a subjective act of the individual. Though he can describe Christ's faithfulness as a kind of power, he rejects any such designation for human faith because of his prior assumption of it as subjective. Yet, if a link could be forged between divine power and human faith, it would open the door to a fresh reading of St. Paul's theology that would transcend the current contrast between justification by faith and participation in Christ.

Assessment

The majority of these scholars look upon faith as a human response that cannot be considered a work of the Law that achieves salvation. It is an act of the individual, but it is not meritorious. It is not an achievement in terms of salvation but it is an acceptance of God's grace. Such faith is described as elicited, evoked, or awakened from within the person. It is the Word of God that does this, or the Holy Spirit that works within the person. Faith is characterized as an act of obedience to God that springs from a free human

---

185. Hung-Sik, "ΠΙΣΤΙΣ in Galatians," 481–82.

186. "It seems unlikely that human faith has soteriological power in Pauline theology. It is probable, therefore, that Christ's faithfulness is an eschatological and apocalyptic power defeating the power of the law (3:13, 23–25; 5:1) and the power of a value system in which the distinction between circumcision and uncircumcision determines and characterizes the Jewish mind-set and community (5:6). . .πίστις denotes Christ's faithfulness as a salvific power, not 'human faith expressing itself through love.'" Hung-Sik, "ΠΙΣΤΙΣ in Galatians," 483–4.

187. Hung-Sik, "ΠΙΣΤΙΣ in Galatians," 487.

will even if the Holy Spirit enables the act. Some scholars come close to resolving such paradoxical descriptions by emphasizing one or the other side of the equation, but agree that faith must be an act of the human person with or without divine assistance. Whether God enables, evokes, or moves one to faith, still, it is the human being, the finite creature that believes in response to God's initiative.

Does faith for St. Paul have a double origin? Can humans be responsible, even in small part, for their own faith? But that makes little sense if one takes seriously St. Paul's rejection of boasting. To have faith is to have justification and salvation. All, according to the Apostle, are gifts of God's grace and cannot be sources of human boasting. Yet, to designate the self as the origin of faith or the self as responsible for faith, is to allow the boast that the self *is* in some measure responsible for one's own salvation. Either faith is a pure gift of God or it is not. If it is not, then human beings are responsible for their own salvation, and works of the law would then become the true path to heaven. This in turn would nullify faith and empty all the promises of God.[188] But St. Paul is adamant about the fact that it is grace that saves, that faith is not a work, and that one may not save oneself by one's own efforts.

Hung-Sik Choi's designation of Christ's faithfulness as an eschatological and apocalyptic power, on the other hand, may lead us on a path that could prove beneficial. But first we must investigate those scholars who, far from emphasizing faith as a human work, see it as a divine gift. Perhaps our search will improve with their insights.

188. Rom 4:14.

3

Faith as Gift and Yet . . .

A NUMBER OF SCHOLARS treat the faith of St. Paul not primarily as a human choice or innate capacity of the individual, but as a gift of God or the Holy Spirit. At the same time, however, many of these authors also retain the language of faith as human act or responsibility.

The Reformers

Martin Luther regarded faith as a gift of God that comes through the Word.

> This is why we continually teach that the knowledge of Christ and of faith is not a human work, but utterly a divine gift; as God creates faith so He preserves us in it. And just as He initially gives us faith through the Word, so later on He exercises, increases, strengthens, and perfects it in us by that Word.[1]

Faith cannot be generated by the human being. "For as no one can give himself faith, neither can he take away his own unbelief."[2]

Faith is transformative and alters the person to whom it is given. "Faith, however, is a divine work in us which changes us and makes us to be born anew of God, John 1[:12–13]. It kills the old Adam and makes us

---

1. Luther, *Lectures on Galatians*, 64. "The true Gospel, however, is this: Works or love are not the ornament or perfection of faith; but faith itself is a gift of God, a work of God in our hearts, which justifies us because it takes hold of Christ as the Savior." LW 26:88.

2. Luther, *Introduction to the New Testament*, 370–71.

altogether different men, in heart and spirit and mind and powers; and it brings with it the Holy Spirit. O it is a living, busy, active, mighty thing, this faith."[3] Faith accomplishes a union with Christ because Christ is "present in the faith itself."[4]

But faith is also very human and can be weak. "But because faith is weak, it is not perfected without the imputation of God. Hence faith begins righteousness, but imputation perfects it until the day of Christ."[5] Faith is imperfect even though it is granted by God.

> For, as I have said, these two things make Christian righteousness perfect: The first is faith in the heart, which is a divinely granted gift and which formally believes in Christ; the second is that God reckons this imperfect faith as perfect righteousness for the sake of Christ, His Son, who suffered for the sins of the world and in whom I begin to believe.[6]

For Luther, faith accomplishes the extraordinary union of the devotee with Christ. "But faith must be taught correctly, namely, that by it you are so cemented to Christ that He and you are as one person, which cannot be separated but remains attached to Him forever and declares: 'I am as Christ.'"[7] It is through faith that one lives in Christ and is "caught up beyond himself into God."[8]

Luther affirmed that "to believe in Christ is to put Him on, to be made one with Him."[9] Faith is therefore an intensely personal and intimate union with Christ and the devotee. This faith has transformed the person from enemy to friend. Luther was clear and consistent in his view of faith as a divine gift, but like so many others he also clearly insisted that it is something very human and imperfect.

John Calvin expressed a similar sentiment when he wrote, "We ought not to separate Christ from ourselves or ourselves from Him."[10] Calvin also denies faith any merit and described it as a divine gift. "What they [Roman Catholics] say of faith might perhaps hold true, were faith itself, which

3. LW 35:370–71.

4. LW 26:129.

5. LW 26:230.

6. LW 26:231.

7. LW 26:168.

8. Luther, *On Christian Liberty*, 62.

9. LW 27:289.

10. Calvin, *Institutes of the Christian Religion*, 1:542; 1:570.

puts us in possession of righteousness, our own. But seeing that it too is the free gift of God, the exception which they introduce is superfluous. Scripture, indeed, removes all doubt on another ground, when it opposes faith to works, to prevent its being classed among merits."[11] Commenting on Abraham in Genesis Calvin writes, "Abraham believed in God: faith was always the gift of the Holy Spirit; therefore God inscribed his covenant in Abraham's heart (Genesis 15:6; Romans 4:3; Ephesians 2:8)."[12]

The two Reformers were clear that faith is a divine gift that did not merit any legal recognition but, however weak it may be within the individual, is still capable of uniting the believer with the object of faith. They did not spell out by what means faith accomplishes such things. But they were convinced that though faith contains a human dimension, it is this gift that accomplished righteousness, not the human being.

Modern Scholars

Adolf Schlatter's groundbreaking work on faith in the New Testament was first published in 1885. He famously asserted that for St. Paul faith could not occur without renunciation of the self and its rights.[13] Such faith is mediated through the Holy Spirit but the Spirit is also received by faith.[14] This faith is not a human work, but is grounded in the gracious will of God.[15] "The believer is not a worker and the worker is not a believer."[16] Faith has

---

11. Calvin, *Acts of the Council of Trent,* 110.

12. Calvin, *Commentary on Ezekiel,* 574.

13 "Somit beginnt das Glauben für Paulus mit einem von jeder Beschränkung befreiten Verzicht auf das eigene Recht und das eigene Leben, der sich auch auf das höchste ewige Ziel des Menschen ersteckt." Schlatter, *Der Glaube,* 324.

14. "Es liegt in der Konsequenz des paulinischen Gedankens, dass die Relation des Glaubens zum Geist doppelt betsimmt wird: der Geist wird durch das Glauben und das Glauben durch den Geist erlangt; d. h. es ist auch hier eine voll personhaft gedachte Gemeinschaft gesetzt, die sich in einem einträchtigen Zusammenwirken beider vollzieht." Schlatter, *Der Glaube,* 365.

15. "Der gutige Wille Gottes ist als anhebende schöpferische Kausalität gedacht. Deswegen ist der Glaube die Weise, wie ihr Empfänger an ihr beteiligt wird: „deshalb aus Glauben, damit nach Gnade," Röm. 4,16, weil das Glauben keine Leistung bildet, die das göttliche Geben durch ihren eigenen Wert begründete." Schlatter, *Der Glaube,* 358.

16. "Der Glaubende ist ein nicht Wirkender, der Wirkender ein nicht Glaubender." Schlatter, *Der Glaube,* 338.

its origin in Christ.[17] It is from this faith that the Christian acquires his or her entire existence.[18] Faith also has its origin in hearing.[19]

Schlatter can also speak of faith in connection with divine power.[20] "The word, which we hear, is God's power (Rom 1:6; 1 Cor 1:18), and that is why our faith has its foundation in the power of God (1 Cor 2:4–5)."[21]

Though Schlatter can write of St. Paul's faith in such terms making it clear that faith's origin is not the individual, still he can describe faith as a movement of the human will. "So that faith is bound to the internal movement of the will and its indispensability is evident."[22] Benjamin Schliesser comments on this point in his summary of Schlatter when he writes that for Schlatter, "The will cannot be excluded from the act of faith, because God's goodness has to be affirmed willingly in order to become a present reality."[23]

Adolf Schlatter therefore exhibits a duality of faith that we have encountered before in terms of divine origin and human effort.

Günther Bornkamm expresses clearly the difficulty of some scholars to come to terms with the issue of faith as divine gift or human responsibility.[24] He describes faith in Paul as "acceptance" of God's saving act in Christ.[25] "As such it is a condition for salvation but not in the sense that men must have succeeded in their resolve to attain it before being allowed to participate in salvation."[26] Faith, Bornkamm claims, is the "renunciation of human accomplishment."[27]

17. "Wie die Werke dem Gesetz gehören also von ihm befohlen und zu seiner Erfüllung getan, so gehört das Glauben mit Christus zusammen, weil es durch ihn entstanden und auf ihn gerichtet ist." Schlatter, *Der Glaube*, 335.

18. "So ist der Glaubende, wie Paulus sehr bezeichnend sagt, „der aus Glauben", ὁ ἐκ πίστεως, weil er mit allem, was er hat, aus dem Glauben heraus ensteht. Dieser hat sich als Prinzip und die Wurzel seiner ganzen Existenz bewährt." Schlatter, *Der Glaube*, 374.

19. "Wie das Gesetz das Werk verlangt und in ihn seine Erfüllung hat, so hat das Glauben seinen Ursprung und Bestand im Hören." Schlatter, *Der Glaube*, 339.

20. "Deshalb verbindet sich mit dem Glauben Kraft: ἐνεδυναμώθη τῇ πίστει, [Rom 4:]20." Schlatter, *Der Glaube*, 346.

21. "Das Wort, das wir hören, ist aber Gottes Kraft, Röm. 1,6. 1 Kor. 1,18, weshalb unser Glaube in Gottes Kraft seinem Grund hat, 1 Kor. 2,4.5." Schlatter, *Der Glaube*, 365.

22. "Damit ist das Glauben mit der innersten Bewegung des Willens verknüpft und seine Unerlässlichkeit ist nachgewiesen." Schlatter, *Der Glaube*, 346.

23. Schliesser, *Abraham's Faith in Romans 4*, 16.

24. Bornkamm, *Paul*.

25. Bornkamm, *Paul*, 141.

26. Bornkamm, *Paul*, 142.

27. Bornkamm, *Paul*, 146.

Yet, Bornkamm also claims that faith in Paul's letters as "Reception and acceptance of this reality, though not achievement and a work, is nevertheless supremely an act—the operation of grace on the believer is not a physical compulsion, nor is its recipient an object with no life of its own, as stone is for the sculptor."[28] Here too Bornkamm is suspended between the two poles of divine grace and human action.

Ernst Käsemann places us on the right path when he describes the righteousness of God in terms of gift and power.[29] He writes of the Giver in the Gift.

> God's power becomes God's gift when it takes possession of us, so to speak, enters into us, so that it can be said in Gal. 2.20, "It is no longer I who live, but Christ who lives in me." This gives us a proper understanding of the double bearing of the genitive construction: the gift which is being bestowed here is never at any time separable from its Giver. It partakes of the character of power, in so far as God himself enters the arena and remains in the arena with it.[30]

Käsemann also insists that the gift of righteousness cannot be separated from human action. "The same Lord who calls us to his service enables us for it and requires us to render it in such a way as to ensure that his gift is passed on."[31] He concludes that the righteousness of God is the power of God that triumphs in the world.[32]

When it comes to faith in the power of God, Käsemann can criticize others for mistaking faith as self-understanding or a human virtue or attitude.[33] But the Apostle Paul did conceive of faith as action, in accor-

28. Bornkamm, *Paul*, 201.

29. Käsemann, *New Testament Questions of Today*. "We take the decisive step along the road to the proper understanding of Paul when, and only when, we grasp the indissoluble connection of power and gift within the conception of the divine righteousness; having done so, we wonder why this finding has not long ago come to be taken for granted." Käsemann, *New Testament Questions*, 174.

30. Käsemann, *New Testament Questions*, 173–74.

31. Käsemann, *New Testament Questions*, 175.

32. "All that we have been saying amounts to this: δικαιοσύνη θεοῦ is for Paul God's sovereignty over the world revealing itself eschatologically in Jesus. And, remembering the Greek root, we may also say that it is the rightful power with which God makes his cause to triumph in the world." Käsemann, *New Testament Questions*, 180.

33. "But misunderstandings of this kind do arise when one starts from the alternative between theology and anthropology, reduces faith to self-understanding and ends up in a liberal-Protestant variant of Christ as the cultic deity who brings the true gnosis to his

dance with his Palestinian Jewish contemporaries. However, faith as action could be misunderstood as a "work," "which Paul wants fundamentally to exclude."[34] Käsemann writes that God's righteousness cannot be considered a gift that is merely transferred to human possession, but rather it is never detached from the Giver.[35] This concept will lead to further important results.

But on the very next page Käsemann writes that faith "in Paul remains primarily a decision of the individual person."[36] He also remarks that people can "allow" God to come to them.[37] Yet, on the other hand, he can say that Jesus is the author of Christian faith.[38]

Thus, Käsemann, though emphasizing faith as God's gracious gift of power in a person's life, is nonetheless still caught between describing faith in terms of divine gift on the one hand, and human decision on the other.

Gerhard Friedrich, writing in honor of and in agreement with Hermann Binder, clearly identifies faith in St. Paul's epistles as that which comes from and is an "action of God."[39] In an effort to build upon Binder's work, Friedrich explores the connection between faith and proclamation. Commenting on Romans 10:17, he remarks that it is the proclamation of the gospel that produces faith, not the inner man.[40] The Apostle Paul does not understand faith as a human decision, as evidenced by the fact

---

people." Käsemann, *Perspectives on Paul*, 77, n. 27.

34. Käsemann, *Perspectives on Paul*, 82.

35. "Nor, on the other hand, did he permit righteousness to be considered a gift which could be detached from the giver and transferred to our possession." Käsemann, *Perspectives on Paul*, 82. See also Käsemann, *On Being a Disciple*, 157, where Käsemann makes a similar point.

36. Käsemann, *Perspectives on Paul*, 83.

37. "God comes to us in his promise and makes us righteous—righteous in that we, as the receivers, allow him to come to us." Käsemann, *Perspectives on Paul*, 93.

38. "Jesus becomes in this way again the author of our faith." Käsemann, *Perspectives on Paul*, 100.

39. "Nicht der Mensch ist beim Akt des Glaubens das entscheidende Subjekt, sondern der Glaube ist ein von Gott kommendes Geschehen, einer Aktion Gottes." Friedrich, "Glaube und Verkündigung bei Paulus," 98–99.

40. "Er ruhrt nicht wie ein Samenkorn im Inneren des Menschen, das durch Einflüsse von aussen zum Keimen, Wachsen und Ausreifen kommt, sondern der Glaube entsteht durch die Proklamation des Evangeliums von den Heilstaten Gottes in Jesus Christus. Es wirkt den Glauben wie es auch neue Menschen schafft (1 Kor 4,15)." Friedrich, "Glaube und Verkündigung bei Paulus," 107.

that nowhere in his extant letters does he command faith of his listeners.[41] Rather, "Faith is a grasping by which one is grasped (Phil 3:12), a knowing by which one is known (Gal 4:9), an act by which one is acted upon (Phil 2:12f.)."[42] Faith is a gift of God's grace.[43]

At the same time, however, Friedrich writes of faith as something that proclamation "awakens."[44] He can also describe faith as an act of the human being.[45] Friedrich, therefore, as other scholars we have seen, is caught in the difficulty of trying to describe the dual nature of faith as divine and human simultaneously. But if not a contradiction in essence, is it not a contradiction in terms to describe faith as a gift at the same time as an awakened capacity? If faith has its genesis in the proclamation, how can it be described as being awakened from within the individual? This is the dilemma that seems to hang over so many scholars as they struggle to be faithful to the text of St. Paul's letters.

Peter Stuhlmacher is caught in the same position as we have seen with Mundle and Bultmann. He regards faith as a gift of the Holy Spirit:

> Faith is for Paul the *quintessence of trust in God*. People cannot force this trust to develop by their own efforts, but faith comes from hearing the gospel and is a gift of the Holy Spirit (cf. Gal 3:2; Rom 10:17). . . . *Therefore, justification by faith alone is justification by virtue of the grace of God alone, which opens to people the saving way of faith and gives them the power to live this way by the Holy Spirit.*[46]

For Stuhlmacher then, faith is a trust that cannot come from one's own effort but is a powerful gift of the Holy Spirit.

---

41. "Weil der Glaube nicht eine Entscheidung ist, die der Mensch zu fällen hat, scheint Paulus bei seiner Missionspredigt nie den Imperativ „Glaubet!" verwendet zu haben." Friedrich, "Glaube und Verkündigung bei Paulus," 111.

42. "Der Glaube ist ein Ergreifen, nachdem man ergriffen ist (Phil 3,12), ein Erkennen, nachdem man erkannt ist (Gal 4,9), ein Wirken, das gewirkt ist (Phil 2,12f)." Friedrich, "Glaube und Verkündigung bei Paulus," 111.

43. "Wie wenig der Glaube eine Leistung ist, kann man daran sehen, dass Paulus ihn ein Geschenk der Gnade Gottes nennt (Phil 1,29)." Friedrich, "Glaube und Verkündigung bei Paulus," 111.

44. "Die Verkündigung weckt den Glauben." Friedrich, "Glaube und Verkündigung bei Paulus," 113.

45. "Der Glaube mit dem Herzen ist ein Akt des ganzen Menschen." Friedrich, "Glaube und Verkündigung bei Paulus," 113.

46. Stuhlmacher, *Revisiting Paul's Doctrine*, 65.

On the very next page, however, he writes, "As much as faith is directed toward the Spirit-filled word of God and is not a meritorious human achievement (cf. Rom 10:17 with 2 Cor 4:6; Gal 3:2), one cannot deny that the apostle describes faith as a human act of obedience (cf. Rom 1:5; 6:16–17; 10:16; 15:18; 16:19)."[47] An act of obedience is one that is usually regarded as meritorious. But this cannot be Stuhlmacher's understanding in light of what he had written previously. How does he understand obedience and faith and the interchange or combination of the two?

Stuhlmacher, like so many others, appears caught between describing faith as a gift, while insisting that it is an act of obedience.

Udo Schnelle is consistent in his description of faith as a divine gift.[48] "Faith does not rest on human decision but is a gift of God's grace."[49] This faith is ignited by the gospel and grows out of preaching.[50] "It is not the rhetorical arts of the preacher or the enthusiastic human 'yes' in response that leads to faith but the Spirit and power of God (cf. 1 Cor 2:4–5)."[51]

> The basic structure of the Pauline concept of faith as a saving and thus life-giving power and gift of God shows that it is inappropriate to understand faith as a "condition," "free deed of obedience . . . this sort of decision," "reception and preservation of the message of salvation," "communication process," or "desired human response to the Christian missionary message" or even "to speak of faith as though it had the character of meritorious achievement." Such language does in part name important aspects of the Pauline concept of faith, but at the same time it reverses cause and effect, for it is God's act that first makes faith possible.[52]

This faith must be confessed or it is not faith.[53] But it is not the self that generates faith. Jesus is the genesis of faith.

> Jesus Christ is at one and the same time the one who generates faith and the content of this faith. The center of faith is thus not the believer but the one believed in. Because faith grows out of the

---

47. Stuhlmacher, *Revisiting Paul's Doctrine*, 66.

48. "The Spirit opens the door to faith and the believer then leads his or her life in the power of the Spirit." Schnelle, *Apostle Paul*, 522.

49. Schnelle, *Apostle Paul*, 521.

50. Schnelle, *Apostle Paul*, 522.

51. Schnelle, *Apostle Paul*, 522.

52. Schnelle, *Apostle Paul*, 522–23.

53. "Faith is thus only faith when it is confessed." Schnelle, *Apostle Paul*, 524.

preaching of the gospel, it is ultimately the act of God, grounded only in the Christ event.[54]

Schnelle is entirely consistent in locating the genesis of faith outside the human being and in Jesus Christ. He goes even further, however, and regards faith as a "life-giving power," but does not explain how this power operates in a person's life. Udo Schnelle contributes greatly to understanding the faith of St. Paul as a gift of God.

Moisés Silva describes faith as an act of the individual.[55] But this act is not a meritorious work. "As already pointed out, classical Protestant theology insisted that the Spirit's gift of faith in Christ (= resting completely on God's gracious provision) is excluded from the category of meritorious works."[56] When writing of Galatians, Silva makes clear that though he can describe faith as human response and act, he regards faith as a matter of divine grace:

> But the sad truth that there are people around who misunderstand the nature of the act of believing is hardly a reason to deny that Paul was referring to faith in the phrase πίστις Ἰησοῦ Χριστοῦ. Certainly the Protestant Reformers left no room for ambiguity that such faith was precisely the antithesis of "futile human activity." Indeed, faith is by definition the abandonment of our works and efforts so that we might rest solely on divine grace: οὐ τοῦ θέλοντος οὐδὲ τοῦ τρέχοντος ἀλλὰ τοῦ ἐλεῶντος θεοῦ (Rom 9:16). Thus to say that we are justified not by the works of the law but by faith in Christ is to acknowledge, in the most forceful terms possible, that we must renounce futile human activity and rely on gracious divine initiative. But if so, then the main (theological) motivation for arguing that πίστις Ἰησοῦ Χριστοῦ refers to Christ's own faith(fullness) turns out to be a phantom.[57]

---

54. Schnelle, *Apostle Paul*, 527. "Although for human beings faith is not something they can generate by themselves, it is something that can be lived, experienced, and carried out in one's deeds. Faith thus appears as a creative act of God in human beings, which in turn makes possible human action—indeed demands such action." Schnelle, *Apostle Paul*, 527.

55. Silva, "Faith Versus Works": "individual's believing response," 218; "act of believing," 218; "human response of believing in Christ," 219; "human act," 227; "the Christian's act of believing in Christ," 228; "(2) The prominence of the act of believing," 230; "both Paul and the other NT authors routinely and explicitly speak of faith in God or in Christ as the human response of Christian believers." Silva, "Faith Versus Works," 247.

56. Silva, "Faith Versus Works," 235.

57. Silva, *Faith Versus Works*, 234.

When scholars write of faith in this manner and describe it as an act of the individual or a personal response to God's action in Christ, it is necessary, as Silva does, to explain what they mean by "act" and "response." If they mean that these are independent of the deity and that act and response constitute an innate capacity within the individual from birth, then we may understand that those scholars regard faith as a religious work tantamount to following the Law of Moses. But if they regard this act of faith as something that does not acquire merit before the Lord, then they must also, as Silva does not, explain what that action means within the life of the believer.

Douglas A. Campbell wishes to bridge the divide between confessional faith and participation in Christ in St. Paul's theology by suggesting that the concept of faith, being much more than mere confession, encompasses ethics and therefore must be understood in combination with participation in Christ.[58] He emphasizes that faith is a divine gift.[59] Faith is

> largely coterminous for Paul with Christian thinking as a whole, whether about the nature of God and of Christ—these being captured by its confessional aspects—or appropriate ethical behavior and ministry, but including fundamental Christian moods and postures like joy, peace, and hope. . . . Christian believing is for Paul apparently both comprehensive and ethical, and even emotional; it is an entire mind or mentality.[60]

Faith as a thought process or mentality seems to be an emphasis in Campbell. In fact, joy, peace, and hope are three "mental dynamics [that]

58. "It seems that any complete understanding of belief in Paul must encompass both the gifts of the Spirit concerning that divine father and his son, *and* the gifts of the Spirit in that son, which is really to say that the believing in which Christians participate seems to have a dynamic, Trinitarian structure." Campbell, "Participation," 56.

59. Commenting on Rom 12:3 Campbell writes, "That is, some Christians instantiate grace in the form of prophecy, and are urged to do so in accordance with an underlying gift of faith. That this is a gift of a 'ratio' or '[mathematical] proportion' of faith seems unlikely, however, although this is a possible meaning of the rare ἀναλογία; neither does a reprise of 'the measuring rod of/that is faith' from v. 3 make much sense." Campbell, "Participation," 43. "It seems especially clear then from this additional data that the new Christian mentality of steadfast, rock-like believing in the unseen realities of future resurrection must be a divine gift." Campbell, "Participation," 47. "But it is a realistic and utterly concrete claim and exhortation if Paul views the steadfastly believing Christian mind as a gift of the Holy Spirit, as various clues in some of his texts have already suggested." Campbell, "Participation," 48. "Christians ought to love because Christ's love has been given to them and lives within them. And this is of course the gift of a new mentality or way of thinking, ergo of believing." Campbell, "Participation," 50.

60. Campbell, "Participation," 44.

are all aspects of Christian thinking, which Paul speaks of as Christian believing."[61] This intellectual aspect of faith is something that cannot be forced.[62] Though Campbell is quite clear that he considers faith a gift of the Holy Spirit, he nonetheless insists that "it should be noted immediately that this is emphatically not to exclude a free dimension from an appropriate response by people to revelation."[63] At the same time he wishes to avoid the concept of personal choice when it comes to faith because there exists "a Liberal account of freedom that has done much damage to accurate Christian thinking over the years."[64]

Campbell seems of two minds on the question of faith and participation and is not quite able to achieve his noble goal of combining the two concepts within St. Paul's theology. He cannot overcome the problem of personal responsibility and divine grace because he refuses to release the freedom of assent of the human being to God's gift. Campbell is on to something, however, when he proclaims that faith and participation go together and should not be separated from each other, as so many others who follow Schweitzer do. Faith is an act for Campbell, albeit mental, but one which encompasses both ethical and ecclesial aspects of communal life within the body of Christ.

Michael J. Gorman suggests that a theology of *theosis* exists within St. Paul's letters. "Pauline theology is a theology of theosis—becoming like God by participating in the life of God."[65] He goes further and writes that "God in Christ became what we are so that in Christ we might become what God is, as Paul puts it in 2 Corinthians 5:14–21."[66] Gorman attempts, as others have attempted, to bridge the gap between faith and participation

61. Campbell, "Participation," 42.

62. "Hence the notion of 'faith' or 'believing' captures helpfully both the things believed in or held to be true, and the connotation of an uncoerced response of assent to their declaration, this last being something that notions like 'thinking' or 'knowing' do not suggest so directly, thereby possibly explaining why Paul seems to have preferred faith language over these alternatives." Campbell, "Participation," 38.

63. Campbell, "Participation," 56.

64. Campbell, "Participation," 56.

65. Gorman, *Becoming the Gospel*, 3. "I argue that theosis, when used of Paul, means transformative participation in the kenotic, cruciform character of God through Spirit-enabled conformity to the incarnate, crucified, and resurrected/glorified Christ." Gorman, *Becoming the Gospel*, 14.

66. Gorman, *Becoming the Gospel*, 6. Gorman corrects himself on p. 32 where he writes, "To become the righteousness/justice of God is to be transformed into the image of God, which is to become *like* Christ by being *in* Christ."

in Christ by saying that faith is not merely intellectual assent but that it is "full participation, a comprehensive transformation of conviction, character, and communal affiliation."[67] How this transformation takes place is never completely spelled out, but Gorman insists that for St. Paul faith is "a participatory experience, not a mere cognitive or even affective one."[68]

Yet, he can write about faith as "personal response to the gospel" and baptism as "public expression of the personal response."[69] "And since for Paul faith is not only the initial response of a person to the gospel message, but also a person's ongoing posture of devotion and commitment, the word 'faithfulness' . . . is a better rendering of *pistis* and its cognates than is 'faith,' as we have already suggested."[70] Gorman thus comes very close to realizing a solution to our dilemma, but comes up short because he cannot relinquish the idea of faith being more than a personal response of the devotee.

Benjamin Schliesser's published dissertation provides a summary of various scholars, from Adolf Schlatter to Richard B. Hays, who have written on the faith of St. Paul.[71]

Schliesser's own conclusions are attempts at understanding Pauline faith in a wholistic or cosmic fashion. "[Faith] is an anthropological (subjective), an ecclesiological (intersubjective) and a salvation-historical (trans-subjective) concept."[72] He writes of faith as a sphere of power (*die Machtsphäre*) within which believers participate.[73] "This new reality of faith that came with Christ is understood as a category whose purpose is to transfer its salvific power to human beings (3:27–31). In other words, it calls for participation in its salvation-bringing realm, in which God works

---

67. Gorman, *Becoming the Gospel*, 23. Commenting on Rom 6 Gorman writes, "If this is what happens to those who believe the gospel and are baptized, then the very meaning of belief, or faith, has implicitly shifted from a notion of assent or even trust to one of participation: of transferal from one realm to another. It is an understanding of faith as embrace—or better yet, of being embraced, even enveloped." Gorman, *Becoming the Gospel*, 27.

68. Gorman, *Becoming the Gospel*, 28.

69. Gorman, *Becoming the Gospel*, 28.

70. Gorman, *Becoming the Gospel*, 92.

71. Schliesser, *Abraham's Faith*.

72. Schliesser, *Abraham's Faith*, 392–93.

73. "One has to take seriously the global salvation-historical dimension of faith as 'Machtsphäre,' but also the character of the gospel as δύναμις θεοῦ, which calls human beings into this sphere." Schliesser, *Abraham's Faith*, 397. "If πίστις is powerful sphere [*sic*], it also has an authority and a claim to include and involve people." Schliesser, *Abraham's Faith*, 399.

justification."[74] Commenting on Rom 1:17 he writes, "'From faith to faith' means that our faith is the consequence of God's act of salvation, the mode of participation therein."[75] This powerful sphere "has an authority and a claim to include and involve people."[76] Pauline theology is properly characterized as "first, humankind before and apart from πίστις, and second, the reality of and participation in the divinely established πίστις."[77] The concept of faith has a universal and individual dimension that incorporate both "God's action and human faith, for it is God who has established the eschatological reality of faith, which is transferred to us."[78] Quoting Francis Watson, Schliesser writes, "The meaning of faith for Paul 'includes not just "belief" or "trust" in a narrow sense, but the acceptance of a new way of life, with all the beliefs, ethical norms and social reorientation which this entails.'"[79]

In *What Is Faith? (Was ist Glaube?)* Schliesser posits the concept of "emergence" as a way to understand faith.[80] "This model has been used for decades in the natural and human sciences and shows that fundamental changes in complex systems . . . occur in spontaneous, eventful and chaotic leaps."[81] The new configuration of such a system is neither predictable nor inferential. It is at such times that the "discovery of faith" arises.[82]

Though Schliesser accepts the Reformation understanding of faith as *fides creatrix*, still he describes it in terms of an emergence or development within the person. As such, it has at least a modicum of continuity with the old Adam, which Schliesser seems to allow. If that is so, then it also allows the old Adam to claim some ground before God and insist that he had something to do with the development of his own salvation.

Schliesser is right to point out the multi-dimensional aspect of faith and that it is not merely human invention but rather a sphere of divine

74. Schliesser, *Abraham's Faith*, 394.

75. Schliesser, *Abraham's Faith*, 397–97.

76. Schliesser, *Abraham's Faith*, 399.

77. Schliesser, *Abraham's Faith*, 401.

78. Schliesser, *Abraham's Faith*, 406.

79. Schliesser, *Abraham's Faith*, 409.

80. Schliesser, *Was ist Glaube?*

81. "Dieses Modell kommt seit einigen Jahrzehnten in den Natur- und Humanwissenschaften zur Anwendung und zeigt, "dass grundsätzlich Veränderungen in komplexen Systemen . . . in spontanen, ereignishaften und 'chaotischen' Sprüngen geschehen.'" Schliesser, *Was ist Glaube?*, 116.

82. Schliesser, *Was ist Glaube?*, 116.

power that envelops the individual. However, he does not extend this aspect toward the transformation of the person but only mentions participation, involvement, transference, or emergence. These concepts are meaningful, but they do not go far enough because they do not describe a total transformation of the person from one existence to another, which St. Paul describes. They do not denote the refashioning of the person, or what St. Paul terms a "new creation."[83] It is only with the language of transformation, I contend, that one adequately describes what St. Paul means by faith.

Assessment

These scholars have advanced an understanding of faith as a gift that provides a clearer path to solving the dilemma we have been dealing with. Yet, how does one reconcile the assertion that faith can be a gift of God and at the same time a free verdict of the human heart? The Reformers did not explain their concept of faith, but subsequent scholars have tried to delve deeper into the subject with some interesting results. Each of these scholars has emphasized faith as gift, yet some have gone further. Ernst Käsemann understands that what gifts God gives are not merely self-contained events but ones that are never separated from the Giver. The idea that the Giver is in the gift can help transform our thinking and yield significant results. Udo Schnelle, in turn, regards faith as a "life-giving power" and Campbell and Gorman allow that faith in Christ and participation in Christ go together. Benjamin Schliesser stands upon the shoulders of those previous theologians and takes us further down the road with his concept of emergence and faith as multidimensional. But it is his identification of faith as a sphere of power within which the believer resides that takes us to the point at which we must now return to the source if we are to resolve the issue.

---

83. 2 Cor 5:17; Gal 6:15.

4

The Objectified Noun and Human Faith
in the Letters of St. Paul

The Objectified Noun and the Adjective

ON OCCASION ST. PAUL will employ πίστις in the form of an objectified noun signifying the content of faith. He also uses πιστός to identify a person who is faithful.[1]

Toward the end of chapter one in Philippians St. Paul expresses his ambivalence concerning his own life and death, concluding that he will remain in the flesh for the sake of the Philippians and further their "progress and joy in the faith."[2] He instructs them to stand firm in the same mind and spirit "striving side by side for the faith of the gospel."[3] In Gal 1:23 he writes about "the faith" that he had once persecuted but had begun to preach after his conversion. In Romans he writes of "the word of faith that we preach."[4] In 1 Cor 13:7 he also writes about love as an objectified attribute that "bears all things, believes all things, hopes all things, endures all things."

---

1. 1 Cor 1:9; 4:2, 17; 7:25; 10:13; 11:18; 2 Cor 1:18; 6:15; Gal 3:9; 1 Thess 5:24.
2. Phil 1:25.
3. Phil 2:27.
4. Rom 10:8.

The Apostle is also aware of the adjective πιστός (faithful) and uses it to describe a positive quality of God in Romans 5:24.[5] He uses the term to describe both God and human beings in the Corinthian correspondence, Galatians, and 1 Thessalonians.[6]

Human Faith

A facile reading of St. Paul's epistles yields the obvious conclusion that the Apostle thinks people actually do believe.[7] He will often use the first or second person of the verb "to believe" because he thinks that faith is something that human beings themselves practice. It is, therefore, of little surprise that numerous readers of the Apostle assume that the faith of St. Paul is a human work. Many such passages are self-explanatory but a few require comment.

1 Thessalonians

1 Thessalonians is the oldest extant letter from the Apostle Paul. It was written to a new community of Christians in Macedonia that seemed to suffer from a lack of eschatological hope.

1:6–7—"*And you became imitators of us and the Lord, receiving the word in much distress with the joy of the Holy Spirit so that you became an example to all the believers in Macedonia and in Achaia.*"[8]

This is the first reference to believers in St. Paul's letters. Some may wish to contend that the participle, τοῖς πιστεύουσιν, indicates a human act by pointing out that the Apostle is indeed referring to people. It is undeniable that people do the believing that St. Paul writes of. Yet, when we refer to our existence, or our lives, we do not thereby indicate that we created ourselves or that we gave birth to ourselves. We merely convey the thought that the center of our being, our identity, has to do with the fact of existence and life. Likewise, when the Apostle identifies people as "believers" he is not thereby assuming that they have created their faith, only that they have

5. "The One who called you is faithful and he will do it."

6. 1 Cor 1:9; 4:2, 17; 7:25; 10:13; 2 Cor 1:18; 6:15; Gal 3:9; 1 Thess 5:24.

7. See Gal 2:16; 3:6–9, 22–27; 6:10; 1 Cor 1:21; 2:5; 3:5; 11:18; 14:22; 15:2, 11, 14, 17; 2 Cor 1:24; 8:7; 10:15; Rom 1:8, 12, 16–17; 3:2–3, 21–22, 25–28; 4:3–5, 11, 16–20, 24; 5:1–2; 6:8; 9:30–33; 10:4, 9–11, 14–17; 13:11; 14:1, 2, 22–23; 15:13; 16:26.

8. All translations are the author's.

a relational identity toward God that is characterized by belief. A number of passages in 1 Thessalonians that contain πίστις fall within this relational category.[9]

2:13—*"but just as it is truly the word of God, which is also at work in you believers."*

This is a reference to personal faith, but there is something of power or work connected to that faith. It is God's word that works in the believers.[10] The question is what work is being done? Does faith constitute the working or are those who already believe energized for some other task? Since there is no other reference in the phrase to another activity other than faith, it seems likely that faith is actually what is being worked. If so, then faith is the result of the energizing word of God. The word gives people the power to believe, which is quite in keeping with Paul's earlier statement in verse four that God grants prior approval before faith is possible. In any case, the Apostle has coupled divine work and human faith in the same breath. Not only that, but the present tense of the verb denotes a continuous action that has yet to end. The Word is not a momentary energy in the mind of the Apostle but rather an ongoing work that persistently works in the believers.

Philemon

Philemon was written to an individual friend of St. Paul whose slave had run away and somehow found his way to the Apostle's jail cell. Paul cajoles his friend by not so subtle means so that he might treat the runaway with mercy. He begins his short letter by thanking God in verses five and six: *"because I hear of your love and of the faith that you have toward the Lord Jesus and for all the saints, so that the fellowship of your faith be effective in the knowledge of all the good that is in us for Christ."*[11]

In the phrase, ἡ κοινωνία τῆς πίστεως, Paul must be referring to the effects of love and faith, not the attributes themselves. If the meaning is "fellowship of faith" it must refer to the camaraderie that faith produces. Or, if the translation is "sharing of your faith"[12] then it refers to the effect of the verbal expression on others of what one believes. Either way, faith is communally active and faith can become effective. It can be "at work" in

9. See 1 Thess 1:8; 2:10; 3:2, 5, 6, 7; 4:14.

10. See chapter six below on Faith as Power.

11. Phlm 5–6.

12. NRSV.

the world and produce results. Thus, personal faith in Philemon is an active attribute that produces certain effects. The Apostle, presumably, wishes that such faith will produce mercy in Philemon so that he will treat the runaway slave as well as he treats St. Paul.[13]

Philippians

A curious mention of human faith in Philippians 2:17 occurs in a complex sentence replete with metaphor. Paul speaks of being "poured out as a libation" on the altar and "λειτουργία" of faith. The NRSV has "being poured out as a libation over the sacrifice and the offering of your faith." The ESV has "poured out as a drink offering upon the sacrificial offering of your faith." Both translations assume that faith is something that the human offers to God.[14] But the NIV has "sacrifice and service coming from your faith." The latter seems preferable as a genitive of source that avoids a host of theological pitfalls and fits well with St. Paul's consistent witness that people have nothing to offer God, but that they receive everything from God (See 1 Cor 4:7).

1 Corinthians

1 Corinthians was written in response to an inquiry from the Corinthian congregation and addressed issues that hampered its fellowship. Toward the end of the letter Paul writes,

15:11—*"Whether therefore it was I or they, thus we preached and thus you believed."*

Preaching precedes human faith and determines it. The content of St. Paul's preaching and that of others issued in the fact and content of the Corinthians' faith. As we have encountered before and will again, the Word is prior to and determines the character of faith.

13. See v. 17.
14. See Fowl, *Philippians*, 128–29.

2 Corinthians

2 Corinthians was written on the occasion of St. Paul's collection for the relief of the Church in Palestine, and concerning his ongoing difficulties with that congregation.

4:13—*"Having the same spirit of faith according to what is written, "I believed, therefore I spoke," we also believe and so have spoken."*

St. Paul is writing of human faith, but it is a faith that has a special quality in connection to scripture. Just as the Psalmist believed and spoke, so does Paul. He is connecting his faith with that of the Psalmist and claiming to have the same spirit. This is not possible unless the Apostle considers faith as something that can reach across the centuries. It is human faith to be sure, but it has a special quality of a timeless spirit attached to it. Moreover, it is this same spirit of faith that is now connected to a gospel message.

5:7—*"For we walk by faith, not by sight."*

Faith is the means or agent whereby St. Paul and his fellow Christians live. However one may construe the nature of faith in this passage, it is something that propels the believer to behave in a certain way. Faith, for the Apostle, determines one's manner of life.

Romans

The letter to the Romans was written to a church the Apostle had not yet visited, but one which he had hoped would send him on his way to Spain. He addresses the fact of sin across all human distinctions in the first three chapters.

3:2–3—*"First, because they were entrusted with the oracles of God. What then, if some did not believe, does their unbelief nullify faith in God?"*

St. Paul here writes of the Jews and their priority in God's economy, declaring that they had been "entrusted" with the oracles of God. The Apostle means to convey the thought that the Jews had been given something that they did not acquire for themselves. The oracles of God were a gift.

The next verse is instructive, however, because it says, "And yet, if some did not believe does their unbelief nullify faith in God?" One may attempt a subjective rendering of faith in the phrase, τὴν πίστιν τοῦ θεοῦ, as "the faithfulness of God," but the context argues against it since Paul is talking about human faith. Only if one translates faith as "faithfulness" could one possibly construe the phrase as subjective, but that is circular reasoning. It would not be an illegitimate grammatical reading, but it is unnecessary because the context more than allows for a reading that emphasizes faith in God, not God's faithfulness. It is perfectly logical to understand the Apostle's meaning as: the unbelief of some people does not nullify other people's faith in God. Only if one decides *a priori* that πίστις means "faithfulness," would one then be compelled to translate this verse as a subjective genitive.[15]

4:18—"*Who beyond all hope believed he would be the father of many nations according to what was spoken, 'Thus will be your seed.'*"

Abraham believed in the future that God had promised him. He believed in something that was not yet real, indeed it was beyond all hope. No wonder so many have considered Paul's Abraham to be a giant of faith. Yet, that faith is still determined by a prior word. That faith followed from something that the Patriarch did not concoct himself. As we have seen and will see again, the external word precedes faith.

6:8—"*But if we have died with Christ, we believe that we will also live with him.*"

Once again we encounter a relational verb but it also signifies a profound insight that those who have "died" are capable of belief. How can this be? How can one be "alive to God in Christ Jesus" as verse 11 declares, unless, of course, one has been given a new life in Christ? How are the dead to raise themselves, and can faith be engendered without any divine assistance? For if one believes that one's own human faith is able to acquire all the blessings of God in Christ, then one must also believe that one can raise oneself from the dead. But to believe that is not to believe in God, but in one's own faith. For to regard one's own human faith as the ability to grasp the truth of Christ is the same for Paul as if to claim that one had done away with oneself and resurrected oneself, for the Apostle makes clear that only through death can new life come and that new life cannot come from the dead. But St. Paul witnesses that those who have been given new life may believe by the same power that raised them.

Perhaps someone will object and claim that Paul is speaking metaphorically and that Christians do not actually die in baptism. But this is to rob the Apostle's language of its force and import. If Albert Schweitzer was wrong about faith, he was right about Paul's mysticism. That mysticism

---

15. See Hays, *Faith of Jesus Christ*, 157–61 where Hays justifies his interpretation by asking how human faith "somehow manifests the righteousness of God or proves God's integrity?" Such a question only follows from the assumption that faith is merely human.

is powerfully on display in this verse. If one insists that Paul meant only a metaphorical death, then the Apostle's preaching loses its mystical force.

10:9–11—"*For if you confess with your mouth that Jesus is Lord and believe in your heart that God raised him from the dead, you will be saved. For the heart believes to righteousness, and the mouth confesses to salvation. For scripture says, 'Everyone who believes in him will not be shamed.'*"

St. Paul clearly believes that people believe! They believe with the heart, the center of their being. This means that faith has to do with the ultimate essence of the person and not a mere aspect or trait. St. Paul's point is that faith is at the center of the Christian. If this were the only comment on faith that we had from St. Paul we would be quite within our rights to understand faith as a human ability or capacity that can achieve salvation. Taken in broad context, however, amid his other statements on faith, one must be careful not to make such easy assumptions.

As Gerhard Friedrich states, nowhere does St. Paul command his listeners to believe.[16] If there were a chance for him to deliver such a command, this passage would be the most appropriate. But he does not avail himself of the opportunity because he knows that though the heart believes, it does so by virtue of its transformation through the word of God.

14:22–23—"*The faith that you have according to yourself, have before God. Blessed is the one who does not judge himself by what he approves. The one who doubts if he eats is condemned because it is not from faith. Everything that is not from faith is sin.*"

Faith is characterized as quite personal in this passage. It may even appear to some as a possession. Yet, in this verse faith is a relational condition that is held in the presence of God and is never something divorced from its object. If faith is a possession, then it is a curious one that must always be possessed in the presence of Another.

Paul next remarks that if something is not born of faith, it is sin. Faith is therefore the source of everything good. The phrase that he employs (ἐκ πίστεως) is the exact same phrase that is usually translated in an instrumental fashion ("by faith") in other contexts.[17] But most translators do not translate this passage in an instrumental manner, rather in the manner of source.[18] If the Apostle understands faith as a source in this context, it is not

---

16. Friedrich, "Glaube," 111. See also 1 Cor 9:17 where the Apostle suggests that his whole ministry was not of his own choice.

17. Gal 2, 3. See below the excursus on ἐκ πίστεως, p. 78.

18. RSV, NRSV, NIV, ESV, NKJV, etc. See below the excursus on ἐκ πίστεως.

so far-fetched to translate it in similar fashion in other contexts since in many of those other contexts St. Paul is also writing of human faith.[19]

Conclusion

The faith of St. Paul is a continuous human action that follows from the word of God and determines how one lives one's life. Faith is continuously active and constitutes the relation between Christians and God. There is no dispute that St. Paul thinks people actually do believe. As he clearly states, one believes with the heart. Since the Apostle writes in this manner and treats faith as a human act, it is quite understandable that many assume faith to be a human work. However, as the following passages will show, there is a serious problem with that assumption, at least for the Apostle. For him, faith cannot be reduced to a human attitude, choice, or condition. Even when describing human faith, St. Paul's language betrays a dimension to believing that far exceeds anything human.

19. Rom 1:17; 3:26; 4:16; 5:1; 9:30, 32; 10:6.

5

Faith as Gift in the Letters of St. Paul

THOUGH ST. PAUL CERTAINLY considered faith a human act, he also writes of it as a divine gift, as something bestowed upon the individual. Nowhere, in his extant letters, does St. Paul describe faith as originating with the human being. Instead, the Apostle writes of faith as a fruit or manifestation of the Holy Spirit, something that is apportioned by God. The word of God is the avenue by which faith is given to a person and the advent of faith grants new life.

Faith as Divine Gift

The Apostle, more than once, lists ἡ πίστις as among the gifts of the Holy Spirit. Though one might quibble about the translation of ἡ πίστις in the following verses, one may not claim that ἡ πίστις, however it is translated, is anything other than something bestowed by God.

Galatians

5:22—"*The fruit of the spirit is love, joy, peace, patience, kindness, goodness, faith.*"

The NKJV, ESV, NRSV, and NIV all translate πίστις in this verse as "faithfulness." The KJV translates it merely as "faith." Scholars have contended that ἡ πίστις meant both faith and faithfulness in Hellenistic usage[1] and that in this context πίστις should be translated as faithfulness.[2] Faithfulness carries with it the connotation of obedience, which is decidedly a human activity. That is why many wish to translate πίστις as "faithfulness" in this context because such a translation fits well with the other items on the list which may be classified as abilities exercised by humans.

But what if Paul had meant both here and in a similar list in 1 Corinthians 12 to jar the reader into realizing that faith or believing is just as much a gift of the Spirit as all the other abilities on the list? Each ability on the list is a "fruit" or "manifestation" of the Spirit and must be understood thereby as a product of the Spirit, not the human being. The Apostle is not claiming some innate human ability for all these gifts, but rather that the Spirit has bestowed them on people and as a consequence, people may actually perform them. Faith, or the act of believing, fits very well in such a list as a gift that the Holy Spirit grants and that people actually do practice, just as with the other items on the list. Whether, therefore, one translates πίστις as faith or faithfulness, one must still acknowledge that, for St. Paul, ἡ πίστις is a gift.

Besides, faithfulness requires faith before one may demonstrate that quality in action and life. Perhaps in our rush to make sense of this passage and the one in 1 Cor 12, we have short-changed St. Paul's language and analyzed it too pointedly. The Apostle may well have meant not just faithfulness as something in line with the other behavioral gifts that he lists, but simple Christian faith as well, for it is from faith that faithfulness springs. If St. Paul did not divide the two, perhaps we should not either. In fact, the dividing of faith from faithfulness is a central part of the problem in understanding the faith of St. Paul. It is when faith is separated from faithfulness that readers of the letters of Paul mistake the organic fluidity of believing and living as not only distinct but separated, when they are actually of one piece. In this single term, "faith," we may understand that just as a tree does not bear fruit apart from its branches, so faith produces faithfulness as a natural outgrowth, not as a separate and discreet response enacted by individuals.

---

1. See BAGD, πίστις, εως, ἡ, 818–20; Bultmann, πιστεύω, 217–22; Hooker, "Another Look," 46–62.

2. See LW 27:95, and Betz, *Galatians*, 288. But see Harrisville, *1 Corinthians*, where Harrisville writes that 1 Cor 12:8–10 is "far more suggestive of a quantity than a type of faith," 209.

1 Corinthians

3:5—"*Who then is Apollos? Or who is Paul? Servants through whom you believed and to each as the Lord gave.*"

Faith comes through servants who preach the word. Those servants were endowed by God to impart their service to others. As such, they are not only conduits through which the service came but this service enabled the faith of the Corinthians. Faith is clearly a gift in this passage, for the Apostle writes that the Lord gave them faith. Each received the capacity to believe from the Lord when his servants supplied their service. Whether "to each" refers to Paul and Apollos or the Corinthians, the gift of faith has been bestowed by God and not earned, acquired, or produced by human beings.

12:6–9—"*and there are varieties of activities, but the same God who energizes all in everyone. To each is given the manifestation of the spirit for the common good. For to one, through the spirit, is given a word of wisdom, to another a word of knowledge, according to the same spirit, to another faith, in the same spirit, to another, gifts of healing in the one spirit.*"

St. Paul is enumerating the gifts of the spirit (as he does in Galatians 5:22, above) and one of them is faith. It is therefore unmistakable that he considers 'η πίστις a gift. Even if he considers it one gift among many, it is still a gift, although it is strange that it should appear in this list as though it were an individual gift not bestowed on all. Perhaps Paul means to say that every believer has the gift of faith. Does he include faith in this list because he wants the Corinthians to realize that so-called "special" gifts are just as common and no more important than the faith that every one of them has? It is not inconceivable that the Apostle writes in an ironic fashion to impress upon the Corinthians that faith is just as precious a gift of the Spirit as all the other gifts.

What if we have misunderstood Paul's two lists in Galatians and 1 Corinthians in thinking that each of the "gifts" is something that humans perform by themselves without assistance? Yet, each of the items is "given" not taken, acquired, or seized. Each of the items is a "manifestation of the spirit," not the human being. Each of them is "empowered" by the same Spirit. Therefore, if we are to be consistent according to the context of both lists of gifts, each and every one of the "abilities" on those lists, faith included, are not to be understood as abilities that the human being self-engenders or produces, but rather abilities that are bestowed upon human beings, as gifts.

2 Corinthians

8:7—"But just as you excel in all things, in faith and reason and in knowledge and all zeal and by the love from us among you, may you also excel in this gift."

St. Paul is being sarcastic again and puffing up the Corinthians, telling them that since they excel in all those other gifts (faith among them), they should excel in the gift of charitable giving as well. He includes faith in his list of gifts. Its inclusion seems almost pedestrian, as though faith as gift were an assumption that the Corinthians would easily recognize. As such it signals an assumed understanding between Apostle and congregation that is worthy of note. One may wish to attempt a reading of these gifts as things given by the Corinthians to others, as one gives charity. But since Paul writes of his love to them as one of the gifts, it seems prudent to interpret faith, reason, knowledge and zeal, as divine gifts that have been bestowed upon the Corinthians, to which now the Apostle hopes generosity will be added.

Romans

12:3—"For I say through the grace that has been given to me, to all among you not to think highly beyond which it is necessary to think, but to think with sober judgment, to each as God has apportioned a measure of faith."

Whether one translates μέτρον πίστεως as "measure of faith," "measuring rod consisting of faith," or "measuring rod of faith,"[3] God is the one who apportions it. The faith of St. Paul is clearly apportioned by God, not the human being. This one verse alone is enough to demolish the notion that (for the Apostle at least) faith springs from the individual. Clearly for Paul it does not. God is the source and granter of faith. Time and again Paul wrote of the divine origin of his gospel. How then could his faith, which is the avenue by which salvation comes, be from any other source? Those who wish to argue for faith as a human work in St. Paul's letters must surmount this verse, among others.

3. Jewett, *Romans*, 741.

12:6—*"Having gifts according to the grace that was given you differently, whether prophecy according to the proportion of faith."*

The Apostle continues the same thought from verse three, that faith is apportioned from God. Even if Paul intends to say that faith's proportion determines prophecy, τῆς πίστεως is still contained within the general context of gift.

Faith as divine gift is no passing mention in St. Paul's letters because he repeats the thought here as elsewhere. He seems to be rather consistent in his view on the matter. If so, then scholars must take note of not only the repetition of faith as a gift in St. Paul's letters, but the facile manner in which he writes of it as such, as though it were an assumption to which both he and his readers readily agreed.

Abraham and Faith

St. Paul's exemplary paragon of faith was the patriarch, Abraham. His use of Abraham was maverick and derived from the Pauline understanding of the cross.[4] The manner in which he writes about Abraham's faith is completely in keeping with the understanding of faith as a gift.

Romans

4:3–5—*"For what does scripture say? "Abraham believed God and it was counted to him as righteousness." To the one who works, his pay is not considered a gift but something owed. But to one who does not work but believes the One who justifies the ungodly, his faith is counted as righteousness."*

Verse four introduces the concept of faith as a gift when it contains the phrase κατὰ χάριν. It is clear from the juxtaposition of works and faith, that faith is not a human work. St. Paul's point is that Abraham was not working when he believed. This rules out any thought of faith being something for which the human may take credit. Indeed, as the quotation from Genesis demonstrates, it is God who does the crediting, not the human being. Because this is so, even if people could boast of their faith, they would still not have the ability to credit that faith before God. The hand that writes the credit in the ledger is not human, but divine.

---

4. See Harrisville, *Figure of Abraham.*

When Paul writes that it was "his faith" that was counted as righteous, it does not mean that Abraham owned his faith. Nor can it mean that the Apostle suddenly contradicts himself to claim some human credit for Abraham's faith. Rather, it is merely a pronoun that designates the genitive of description or relation. As such, it does not denote Abraham's responsibility for his faith, only that he believed.

4:11–14—*"And he received the sign of circumcision, a seal of the righteousness of faith while in uncircumcision, so that he is the father of all who believe while uncircumcised, so that righteousness may be counted to them— and the father of the circumcised, to those not of the circumcision only but also those who walk in the footsteps of the faith of our father Abraham while he was uncircumcised. For it was not by means of the law that the promise came to Abraham and to his seed, that he would inherit the world, but through the righteousness of faith. For if the heirs are from the law, faith has been emptied and the promise nullified."*

If we understand faith as a gift, it is easier to understand what St. Paul means when he writes about those who follow in the footsteps of Abraham. If Abraham was not responsible for his own faith but there are those who follow in the footsteps of his faith, St. Paul cannot mean that Abraham's followers are responsible for their faith, but that they too have been given the same gift. Indeed, only through that gift can anyone be made a follower. Therefore, the Apostle is not assuming that one may copy Abraham's faith by oneself, but that anyone can be given the same faith as that of Abraham.

This passage also makes clear that the law and faith, and the law and the promise are not the same. It is yet another juxtaposition of human works and divine gift. The promise and faith cannot come through the law. They must be delivered by God's grace.

4:16—*"Because of this it is from faith[5] in order that it be according to grace, so that the promise be firm to all the seed, not to the one from the law only, but also to the one from the faith of Abraham, who is the father of us all."*

What could be clearer than that Paul understands faith as a gift? Here he insists that the inheritance of Abraham was not through the law but through faith, in order that everyone recognizes that inheritance as a gift. If faith were a work and a human responsibility, then St. Paul could not complete the phrase by writing of grace and gift. Faith is indication that a gift is being bestowed, not a human work performed. Faith is a demonstration of grace and grace comes from God, not humans. Only in this fashion can the

---

5. See the excursus on ἐκ πίστεως below p. 78.

promise be assured, because if faith and grace were human powers, those powers would fail as surely as people sin and die. Finite creatures cannot guarantee a promise beyond the grave, nor can they guarantee any part of their own future. Therefore, it must be God who gives such guarantees through faith, that is, by grace.

Divine Approval

As a matter of course, in order for a gift to be granted, the giver must first decide to give it. Thus, St. Paul writes of God's prior approval of the divine gift of faith.

1 Thessalonians

2:4—*"but just as we have been approved by God to believe the gospel, so we speak, not as pleasing men, but God who approves our hearts."*

The faith of St. Paul is not something that happens without divine approval.[6] The aorist passive infinitive πιστευθῆναι denotes (together with the preposition ὑπὸ), the agency of God by which the Thessalonians have been approved or found worthy. It would appear that God must first approve that people be entrusted with the gospel. But in order to be entrusted of "faithed" with the gospel, is it not necessary that one believe that gospel? If so, then the Apostle is actually assuming that faith requires prior divine approval. The question is whether or not Paul means that people were worthy of the divine approval, as though they exhibited some trait or characteristic that made them worthy to believe, or, more in keeping with the Apostle's theology, whether they were granted the ability to become believers. Regardless, it is clear that God had first to act on a person's heart before human faith in the gospel became possible.

The Coming of Faith

Faith as a divine gift that required prior approval was not something at which the Apostle arrived by spiritual calisthenics. He did not, as people

---

6. The word δοκιμάζω may be translated "to make a critical examination of something . . . *put to the test . . . prove, approve,*" etc. BDAG, 255.

often say, "come to faith." On the contrary, he writes of the coming of faith. It is as though faith were on a journey and the human being the destination.

Galatians

3:22–27—"*but Scripture confined all things under sin in order that the promise, from faith in Jesus Christ, be given to those who believe. Before faith came we were held under law being confined for the coming faith to be revealed, so that the law was our pedagogue until Christ in order that we be made righteous from faith. With the coming of faith no longer are we under a pedagogue. For all are sons of God through faith in Christ Jesus. For as many of you as were baptized into Christ, have put on Christ.*"

Faith is revealed, writes the Apostle. Moreover, revelation obviously has a divine and not an earthly source. Faith also has a temporal dimension, as indicated by the genitive absolute construction. Yet, one might object that "those who believe" are doing the believing, as though faith were something generated by the human being. But St. Paul is well aware that once faith is given it is active in a person's life and becomes the animating force of the Christian.[7] This passage does not need to imply that faith is essentially human, only that humans have faith.

Some understand this passage to mean that "the coming faith" must refer to the advent of Jesus of Nazareth because of the temporal context.[8] The Apostle's language is multivalent here and does not demand only one possible reading but allows that personal faith as divine gift comes with the advent of Christ. St. Paul did not use the name of Jesus in this context, but he did use "the faith." The word may indeed be construed to convey an objectified meaning, but it may also convey the advent of Christian faith itself, which was impossible before the coming of Christ, but now is possible after his appearance. Perhaps St. Paul wrote in this fashion because of the Galatians' perverted theology, which emphasized ritual over piety. If we take St. Paul at his word and do not read a name where a concept is expressed, then instead of limiting our reading of the verse to an historical event, the verse may refer not only to the event but to the gifts unleashed by the event.[9]

7. Gal 2:20.

8. Betz, *Galatians*, 176n120. Wright, *Justification*, 127. Hays, *Faith of Jesus Christ*, 156–61.

9. Richard Hays places quite a bit of emphasis on this passage for his thesis of the faith

External Source

For the Apostle, faith begins elsewhere than in a person's heart. It must if it comes in time and is a gift of the Holy Spirit, as we have seen. Far from describing faith as in internal production of the human being, St. Paul consistently describes it as stemming from an external source.

1 Thessalonians

3:10—*"night and day praying most earnestly to see your face and to complete what is lacking in your faith."*

Does the Apostle mean that the Thessalonians' faith is not yet well-informed and that they need more instruction to understand their faith? Does he mean that the Thessalonians do not have enough faith and that he will supply them with more? Whatever he intends to convey, it is clear that Paul, at least in this instance, understands the completion of faith as something that originates from outside the person. It is not something that one may supply for oneself. It must come from an external source, in this particular case, the Apostle.[10]

1 Corinthians

1:21—*"For since in the wisdom of God the world did not know God through wisdom, it pleased God through the folly of what we preach to save those who believe."*

The foolish proclamation of St. Paul's message saves those who believe. Believing has nothing do to with human wisdom. Rather, believing has something to do with the foolishness of the Christian message. If that

---

of Jesus Christ as a subjective genitive. He does so because he cannot conceive of faith as anything more than a purely human construct. But if faith is a divine gift and much more than merely human, then it is entirely appropriate to interpret the passage as above. See also Schliesser, "'Christ-Faith," 277–300.

10. See also 1 Thess 5:8—"We, being of the day, let us be sober putting on the breast-plate of faith and love and being crowned with hope of salvation." Here faith, love, and salvation are described metaphorically as Christian garments. This type of speech cannot be pressed too hard for precise meanings, but a metaphor that likens faith and love to clothing signals that the Apostle understands these qualities as external coverings that do not come with a person's birth. They need to be put on. See also Gal 3:27 in which baptized Christians put on Christ.

message is so foolish, then no one can believe it apart from the message itself, which has within it the ability to save those who believe. In the previous verse the Apostle has eliminated the "wise," the "debater," and the "wisdom of the cosmos." All these are human capacities and talents that have nothing to do with the Christian message and faith. If the wisest person cannot know God through wisdom, how may one of ordinary intelligence know Him? Intellectual discrimination, which is the goal of the wise man and debater, is a rational category requiring the wisdom to know the difference between good and bad. But if such rational wisdom, according to St. Paul, is not the path to God or salvation, how can anyone advance the notion that humans are able by themselves to believe in such folly? Faith cannot come from human wisdom, acumen, emotion or reason. It has a different source.

Galatians

3:14—"*in order that the blessing of Abraham to the nations happen in Christ Jesus, in order that we receive the promise of the Spirit through faith.*"

Here faith is the agent or means by which something comes. This is consistent with our previous observations of faith as source, which can easily be understood as the means or agency by which the Spirit is received. This does not have to mean that we first produce the avenue by which the Spirit comes to people, but that faith is the source and means of the Spirit's arrival in people's lives. Paul can use διά and ἐκ with πίστεως because both expressions may refer to faith as source and avenue.[11]

The Word and Faith

Faith is not a gift that is given at one moment in time and never repeated. When speaking of faith as a gift, one must not assume that it is like a Christmas present that is given once and then used solely according to the wishes of the recipient, independent of the giver. Rather, faith has its avenue in the Word that is constantly being proclaimed and voiced. It is in that Word, as in a flowing stream, that faith is continually bestowed and never separated from its source.

11. See the excursus below p. 78.

Romans

10:14–17—*"How then will they call upon one whom they have not believed? How will they believe in one whom they have not heard? How will they hear apart from a preacher? How will they preach unless they are sent? As it is written, "How beautiful are the feet of those who spread the good news!" But not all obeyed the gospel. For Isaiah says, "Lord, who has believed our report?" Then faith [is] from hearing and hearing [is] through the word of Christ."*

Faith is not possible without an external word or message. That word actually creates faith. Preaching must, therefore, come first, then hearing, and then only can believing come. It is in the communication of the gospel that faith is formulated and apart from that word there is no faith. Faith is therefore not a human work but the result of the preaching of the word.

The mystery of faith is that many hear, but not all believe. They have not yet been given the gift or they have been denied it or they have resisted it. Even so, St. Paul insists that the genesis of faith is external, not internal. The word is the avenue or source of faith, not people. Whenever we read of faith in Paul's letters, its source is always external to the human. Faith's origin is always divine.

Galatians

3:2, (5)—*"I want to learn only one thing from you—did you receive the Spirit from works of law or from hearing of faith?"*

The NRSV and NIV have "believing what you heard" but the ESV has "hearing with faith." The KJV and NKJV have "the hearing of faith." The latter merely repeats the Greek phrase but the ESV's rendering can mean that hearing employs faith or faith uses hearing. The NRSV and NIV have altered the parallelism of Paul's phraseology and have decided that the persons do the believing, rejecting the possibility of faith as the source of hearing. When the phrase is translated "hearing with faith," it could be construed that hearing is primary and faith secondary. But if it is the other way around, as in "hearing from faith," then faith is the source of hearing.[12]

What seems clear in this passage is that the law appears to be a force or sphere of influence in this passage, which would make sense if it is to be juxtaposed to faith. This comports with the law as the power of sin in 1 Cor 15:56. If the law is a force to be reckoned with, then in order for the

12. See the excursus on ἐκ πίστεως below p. 78.

contrast between law and faith to work effectively, faith must also be a force or sphere of influence.[13] Both work to produce certain abilities. The one produces works while the other produces hearing.

In any case, it seems clear that faith produces hearing as the law produces works. Hearing is what the human can do just as works are what can be done by people, but the law and faith are both from God not the human. If the contrast is to be properly formulated, then faith cannot be a work or a human responsibility since the law, as a gift of God, is also not a human work or responsibility! Faith must be understood as something determined by and given by God, just as the law was. Otherwise, Paul will be comparing apples and oranges and his argument would fail.

Righteousness and Faith

Righteousness is unquestionably a gift in St. Paul's theology. Faith is the means whereby righteousness is conferred. Faith, therefore, must not be a human work, since that would mean that the gift of righteousness is dependent upon human effort.

Philippians

3:9

In a famous passage St. Paul regards his former life as a complete loss in comparison to his relationship with Christ.[14] He wishes to be found in Christ, "not having my righteousness which comes from the law, but that which comes through faith in Christ, the righteousness from God, [which is] upon faith." If righteousness is not his own, that is, if righteousness does not spring from Paul's own being or efforts, then neither may faith be considered a human product, since that would imply that a human work is the avenue of God's gracious righteousness and Paul would be contradicting himself. It is the law that demands human obedience. But if Paul rejects that obedience as the foundation of righteousness and claims faith as the only proper foundation, then faith cannot be considered a human work in obedience to the law. Righteousness comes from God and is founded on faith.

---

13. See Moule, *Idiom Book*, 81, where Moule mentions "the sphere of faith." See also Schliesser, *Abraham's Faith*, where he writes of faith as a "Machtsphäre," 397.

14. Phil 3:8–11.

But just as righteousness is not of human manufacture so too must faith be of a spiritual origin. If faith were a human work it would place Paul in a theological and logical conundrum and the sentence would make no sense. But if we understand that God's righteousness rests on faith (in opposition to works) and not adherence to the law or any other human effort, then the verses not only make sense but express a profound truth of God's grace.

In verse 12 the Apostle writes that he has not seized or obtained the perfection he strives for "but I press on to make it my own, because Christ Jesus has made me his own." This is very much like the earlier instance in 2:12 in which Paul wrote of working out one's salvation because God is at work in the person. Once again he expresses the idea that his ability is made possible only through God's granting of that ability. This is fully in keeping with the sentiment that Paul "can do all things though him who strengthens me."[15] Perhaps it would be better to translate ἐνδυναμοῦντί not as "strengthens" (as though the Lord adds ability to the person's already existing ability), but as "empowers" and thus understand the Apostle to mean that God gives him all the power he needs to do everything he must do as a believer. God, then, empowers the saints to believe, to love, to endure suffering, and to strive to live for righteousness's sake.[16] Is it Paul's understanding that "all things" include his faith as well? If so, then he is expressing the profound thought that Christian life and faith are empowered by the Lord and not by any human engine.

Galatians

2:16—*"knowing that a man is not made righteous from works of law but through faith in Jesus Christ, and we have believed in Christ Jesus in order that we be made righteous from faith in Christ and not from works of law, because from works of law no one will be made righteous."*

Δικαιωθήσεται is in the passive mood. Being made righteous cannot be something that a person declares oneself to be or a condition that one bestows on oneself. It is a gift of God. If this is so, then faith may not be construed as a human attitude manufactured by the person that can be regarded as the currency that earns righteousness, as though one can

15. Phil 4:13.

16. L&N translate the term as "to cause someone to have the ability to do or to experience something—'to make someone able, to give capability to, to enable, to strengthen, to empower.'" L&N, 74.6.

make oneself righteous by exerting his or her own faith. If that were the case, then Paul would have written that God awards us with righteousness because of our faith, or as a reward of faith. Instead, he writes that we are "righteoused" by means of, from, or through faith because πίστεως is in the genitive, not the accusative case. Therefore, if Paul's theology of God's gracious righteousness is to be held together it requires that faith be commensurate with the gift of righteousness and itself understood as a gift. The means of righteousness must fit the ends.

Excursus: ἐκ πίστεως

The preposition ἐκ carries with it the basic notion of separation. Dana and Mantey translate its root meaning as "out of, from within."[17] BDAG designates its root meanings as "from, out of, away from."[18] It lists the phrase ἐκ πίστεως under the category of "γ. of the inner life, etc., fr. which someth. proceeds."[19] Yet, when we look at modern English translations we often find that the phrase, which St. Paul uses often,[20] is not translated "from out of faith" but "by" faith, as though faith were the instrument or agent for something, not the source of something. The ESV, NRSV, and NIV, for instance, all translate ἐκ πίστεως in Gal 2:16 as "by faith." The famous phrase from Hab 2:4, that Paul quotes in Gal 3:11, is similarly translated.[21] This is a valid translation, but perhaps it can be somewhat misleading because the English word "by" does not denote source, as the Greek preposition ἐκ does. But if we try to read the phrase as St. Paul wrote it, crediting the full sense of

17. Dana and Mantey, *Manual Grammar*, 102.

18. BDAG, 295.

19. BDAG, 297. See also BDF, which places it in the category of a Partitive Genitive, 90.

20. The preposition ἐκ is used by Paul in conjunction with πίστεως nineteen times. Nine of those are in Galatians (eleven if we count 3:2 and 5). He employs διά with πίστεως fifteen times. Seven of those times are in Romans.

21. The Hebrew version of Habakkuk 2:4 has *bet* as the attached preposition to the word "faith." According to BDB, 88–91, this preposition has as its primary meaning, "in," "among," or "within." Its secondary meaning is "at" or "by" (denoting proximity) and its tertiary meaning is "with." Could it be that the translators of the LXX used the Greek ἐκ to translate the Hebrew *bet* in an effort to relate both source (in the sense of "in") and instrumentality? As with the German, *aus*, which is very often used to translate the same word and phrase (See *Die Bibel, Nach der Übersetzung Martin Luthers*, 1984. Rom 1:17; Gal 3:11–12.), and which denotes both source and instrumentality, perhaps the Greek ἐκ was employed to denote the same understanding.

ἐκ, we must retain something of the sense of faith as a source or origin of righteousness, not just as instrument or means.

The difference is important because when the word "by" is used to translate such an important phrase it can mislead the average reader to think that faith is some kind of tool that a person wields in order to complete a task, in this case—righteousness. But that would imply that the person is responsible for the use of the tool, and thus for the completion of the task of righteousness. But, as we have pointed out before, the Apostle to the Gentiles will have none of that. He will not allow any hint of human boasting or responsibility for salvation and therefore it would be self-contradictory had he meant to write that people used faith to finish the job *by* themselves.

The reason for translating the phrase in such a misleading manner is, perhaps, that the translators assume that faith is a human responsibility and naturally and logically wish to convey that assumption in the translation of ἐκ πίστεως.

But if we were to translate the phrase not "by" faith but "from" faith, it would give us a more complete understanding of faith in St. Paul's letters. The English preposition "from" can convey the idea of instrumentality and means but it also conveys the idea of source. Instead of saying that the righteous live "by" faith, we would say that the righteous live "from" faith. This denotes faith not as a tool under the power of the person, but faith as the source of the righteous person's life, so that faith is understood not as a separate instrument by which life is lived, but rather as the source of righteousness. This would not make sense if faith were understood as a human responsibility. On the other hand, if faith is understood as a gift of God then it makes perfect sense to understand faith as source and not as a tool for which people are themselves responsible.

Romans

3:21–22—*"But now, apart from law, the righteousness of God is revealed, moreover it is witnessed to by the law and the prophets, the righteousness of God through faith in Jesus Christ to all who believe."*

In these transitional verses when St. Paul wishes to turn his attention from sin to salvation, righteousness and faith are as closely tied to each other as is a destination to its path. The law, however, is excluded from this path because its performance is not based on revelation or grace but on works. Righteousness, as St. Paul makes clear in 5:17, is a divine gift. If faith is tied to that gift as the means by which the gift of righteousness comes, faith cannot be anything other than a gift itself or it would fall under the incongruent category of human works, which would empty St. Paul's theology of its basic thrust.

3:25–28—*"Whom God put forward as a restoration of good will through faith in his blood, as a demonstration of his righteousness (through the forgiveness of former sins, in the forbearance of God!), to demonstrate his righteousness in the present time that he is righteous and that he justifies the one from faith in Jesus. Where then is boasting? It is excluded! Through what law? That of works? No, but through the law of faith; for we consider that a person is justified with faith, apart from works of law."*

Πίστις denotes human faith in this passage. But it is plainly contrasted to works of law, so it cannot be counted among human achievements.

In verse 27 faith and law (obedience) are tied together in ironic fashion. The language is close to that of Gal 3:2–5 in which the Apostle juxtaposes works of law and hearing of faith. In this passage he mentions a law that is connected to faith. But this must be a vastly different law from that connected to works. Boasting is the difference. One may boast of works of the law, but not of faith. The reason is that faith is of a divine character and origin, whereas works are strictly human, so that one may not boast of the former, only the latter.

The dative form of πίστις in verse 28 may be translated as an instrumental dative ("by faith") as is often the case. But it may also be translated as a dative of respect or association: "with faith." This avoids any mistake that faith is under the power and control of the individual.

Furthermore, it would be cognitively dissonant to suggest that St. Paul avoids human boasting, while at the same time asserting that a human engendered faith is the means whereby people claim divine justification. Faith is indeed the means whereby justification is reckoned, but that reckoning is not of human origin, it is divine. If the reckoning and the justification are both divine, how could it be that the means whereby each is accomplished is through human power? But St. Paul rejects any and all such views. It is better to understand this dative form of πίστις as that divine gift, like breathing, which is given to the Christian whereby he or she may be connected to the justification that the Almighty graciously bestows. Such a rendering fits well with the context of the passage in which the Apostle is at pains to avoid anything that might allow human boasting.

3:30–31—*"since God is the one who justifies the circumcised from faith and the uncircumcised through faith. Therefore, do we nullify the law through faith? Certainly not! On the contrary, we uphold it."*

It is unnecessary to translate faith in this passage as something wholly human. If one understands faith here as the means by which God justifies, as in the former passage, then faith can be understood as a divine avenue through which justification comes, not a human avenue. Besides, how would one nullify a divine law? Would it be through human means? Certainly not! If there were a divine law that could be nullified, it would have to be nullified by a divine means, not human. Therefore, when St. Paul asks if we nullify the law through faith, he does not mean a human work of faith, but the divine avenue of faith that is given to humans. It is through this faith that humans realize the propriety of the law and do not do away with it. But such awareness is not produced by human effort, but by divine gift.

5:1–2—*"Having been justified therefore from faith, we have peace with God through our Lord Jesus Christ, through whom we have also gained access by faith to this grace in which we stand and we boast in hope of the glory of God."*

Peace with God is obtained from the justification that comes from faith and it is from this same faith that access to God's grace is given and in which Christians live. Faith, therefore, brings with it justification and grace. Moreover, it enables the Christian to boast of a future glory. All these things are gained from faith. Yet, how can such marvelous and divine benefits be gained through the act or attitude of a finite being with limited understanding and a sinful proclivity? Does the Apostle mean to relate that a purely human product of the mind and heart can achieve such wonders? But grace cannot be achieved. Its very nature precludes such a thought. That the mention of faith in this passage is surrounded by divine gifts and that this mention follows directly on the heels of chapter 4 in which faith is understood as a gift, the Apostle cannot now incongruently mention faith as a human work or attitude.

Conclusion

If Christian faith can be characterized as a human work in other Christian writers, it cannot be so construed in the Apostle's letters. For St. Paul, faith is a gift of the Holy Spirit, something apportioned by God, approved by the Almighty in which, by which, and from which a person lives. One does not "come to faith." Rather, faith comes to the individual. Works of the law are consistently contrasted to faith in Christ, which demonstrates St. Paul's firm theological stance against understanding faith as a meritorious work. Instead, he lists it among the Spirit's fruits/gifts in Galatians and 1 Corinthians. Moreover, nowhere does the Apostle indicate that faith is of human production or manufacture. Though he writes that people believe, curiously he never credits himself or others with the responsibility of having engendered such faith. It is clear therefore that the faith of St. Paul is a divine gift.

In addition, it should be asked what kind of gift faith is. Most gifts that people give to one another are material gifts that may be meant for single or lasting use by the recipient. For example, someone may receive a basketball as a gift. That person then has control over the gift and uses the gift when and where that person chooses. The giver has no control over how the gift is used. But it is not a material gift that St. Paul speaks of when he writes of the gift of faith. In fact faith, though practiced by the believer, should not be assumed to be a gift that is divorced from its object. That object is God, who bestowed the gift of faith in the first place. Ernst Käsemann's insight that the *Giver* is in the gift, though he was writing of righteousness, is instructive here. If the gift of faith is a singular occurrence in time that subsequently is under the control of the recipient, then the common assumption that faith is a human responsibility would be valid. But if this gift is never divorced from the *Giver*, if it is never disconnected from its object, but is rather something that is continually bestowed by the deity, then it is an extraordinarily different sort of gift, which requires further investigation.

Not only this, but how are we to reconcile the view of faith as gift with those passages in which the Apostle clearly understands faith as a capacity in the individual? How can St. Paul maintain that "we believe," but that such faith is a gift? It seems a contradiction of fatal proportions to write in such a fashion. But if there is a further dimension to faith, a dimension that is dynamic, then perhaps this apparent contradiction can be overcome.

6

Faith as Power in the Letters of St. Paul

IF WE ARE TO solve the dilemma of how St. Paul can write of faith as a human act and yet as a gift of the Spirit, we must draw upon certain passages that represent faith as something more than a human attitude or frame of mind. When we do we find that faith is a transforming power that not only changes hearts and minds, but does so continually.

1 Thessalonians

1 Thessalonians is the oldest extant letter from the Apostle Paul. It was written to a new community of Christians in Macedonia, which seemed to suffer from a lack of eschatological hope. Paul, Silvanus, and Timothy write first to express their thanks to God for the Thessalonian Church. They recall the Thessalonians' "work of faith and labor of love and patience of hope in our Lord Jesus Christ" (1:3).

St. Paul's use of the word πίστις occurs early in the letter as part of the phrase "τοῦ ἔργου τῆς πίστεως," which is a genitival construction that occasions several possible readings. In this case we may rule out such constructions as the possessive genitive, the genitive absolute or the adverbial genitive. It could legitimately be translated as an appositional genitive and understood as though faith is a human work for which St. Paul commends the Thessalonians. The possessive pronoun "your" would tend to lend weight to such a reading. However, as we have already established, the Apostle is quite clear that he does not regard faith as a human work of any

83

sort. It is apparently not a subjective or objective genitive since no personal actor is indicated in the phrase itself. It could be taken as a general genitive of description since there is no preposition in the phrase and since this class of genitive is rather basic to the entire syntactical category.

However, if one were to translate the phrase as a genitive or ablative of source it would fit rather well with the following expressions that could easily signify the sources from which come labor and patience ("labor of love" and "patience of hope"). Faith would then be understood as producing "work" just as love produces labor and hope produces patience. If we read the phrase in this manner, St. Paul and his coworkers here express the idea that the work that the Thessalonians have done springs from faith. The Apostle would then be expressing the thought that faith is the source of energy or work.[1] As such, it cannot be considered a mere human attitude or decision, but something powerful enough to produce good works.

Galatians

3:5 — "Therefore, the one who supplies you with the Spirit and works of power in you [is it] from works of law or from hearing of faith?"

The Spirit and works of power (whether Paul means miracles or not), are associated with hearing and faith. God supplies both. Faith is the avenue through which God supplies such marvels. Is it therefore rational to regard faith as a human construct that has the capacity to accommodate the kind of traffic that the divine delivers? Does Paul actually mean that humans are strong enough to hold the door open for the Spirit and miracles, not once but continuously?[2] That seems a burden too large for any individual

---

1. 2 Thess 1:11 contains a similar phrase ("work of faith") that is complimented by the phrase ἐν δυνάμει. Has the author of 2 Thessalonians, especially if it is the Apostle himself, gone a step further to associate faith with power? The NRSV has "by his power," which construes the phrase ἐν δυνάμει as distributive, referring to the call of God and "every good resolve" in the rest of the verse. But this does not lessen the connection between "in power" and "work of faith," especially since these phrases are juxtaposed to one another. Therefore, we may entertain the intriguing notion that the phrase "work of faith" in 2 Thessalonians carries with it the close association of power. This makes perfect sense if faith is understood as the source of Christian work. If faith is somehow connected to power, then it is easily understood as the source of Christian works. Whether the phrase in 1 Thessalonians carries this attachment to power is another matter. If the Apostle Paul is the author of both epistles, then perhaps we might transfer the meaning of the one phrase to the other. But this is only intriguing conjecture.

2. This is what Bultmann declared. See above, pp. 13–15.

to bear. Or, does he mean that faith is a divine conduit through which God supplies the Spirit and powers? No matter what Paul might mean here, he does convey the thought that divine marvels are to be associated with faith. He has made a concrete connection between faith and energy, or power.[3]

5:5–6—"*For we by the spirit from faith eagerly await the hope of righteousness. For in Christ Jesus neither circumcision strengthens anything nor un-circumcision but faith working through love.*"

St. Paul here portrays the spirit as that which comes from the gift of faith. He can mean the Holy Spirit or another spirit that stems from faith. Either will do since he had earlier written in 3:14 that the Spirit was to be received through faith.

In this passage faith is the source of love's power. Faith energizes love. Faith makes love happen. Paul regards faith as "living and active"[4] not just an attitude or disposition. It is not a momentary choice but an ongoing power that results in acts of love. This verse drives home the thought that faith is not a static quality but a continual force and power for good.

1 Corinthians

2:5—"*in order that your faith not be in the wisdom of men but in the power of God.*"

Human faith is directly linked here with God's power. The previous verse says that St. Paul's word and kerygma are in power and spirit. Can Paul mean that Christians believe in God's power as a circumlocution for Jesus, or that the Corinthians believe the power of the message about Jesus? Whichever it is, faith in Christ is faith in divine power, not human reason. Faith, for Paul, is not based upon human philosophy or mental capacity but upon divine power.

13:2—"*And if I have prophetic ability and know all mysteries and all knowledge and if I have all faith so that I am able to remove mountains, but have no love, I am nothing.*"

The famous chapter 13 begins with a portrayal of virtuous abilities that are compared to the more exalted one of love. St. Paul's goal in 1 Corinthians is to bring the Corinthian church back to reality by teaching them

---

3. Gal 2:8–9 reflects a similar thought concerning the divine supply of power. God energized Paul and Peter with faith in order to perform their assigned tasks. Faith was the power of God that energized both Apostles.

4. LW 35:370–71.

that they have not yet been transported to the realm of the spirit but still live in the real world. That real world needs the real love of Christ and Christians, not the mistaken aggrandizement of personal spiritual gifts, which the Corinthians seem to have emphasized. The Apostle, in this passage, is not denigrating prophecy, knowledge, and faith, but he is telling the Corinthians that such spiritual abilities must always be connected to and result in real love of one's neighbors or they are emptied of any worth. He does not mean to say that love stands apart from prophecy, knowledge, and faith, but that those gifts ought to result in love.[5]

At the end of the chapter he lists faith, hope, and love, with the latter as the greatest. This is because he knows that in the kingdom of heaven faith and hope will be unnecessary since they are only for this life and will not be needed in heaven when believers will behold God face to face. Therefore, when commenting on faith in chapter 13, we should be careful to recognize its temporal worth, while at the same time marveling at its terrestrial significance for the life of the believer in the here and now.

In this context the Apostle astoundingly claims that faith produces the ability to move mountains.[6] If so, then faith cannot be a mere attitude, decision, or disposition within the human heart but a power or force capable of changing the very landscape. It cannot be a mere psychological or emotional quality, but rather an energy that manifests itself by altering geography! Whatever faith is, in St. Paul's theology it is repeatedly linked with power, but here it actually manifests itself in an amazing ability. The Apostle nowhere implies that such faith is a production of the human being. Nowhere will we find any reference to faith as a human manufacture. Rather, as we have seen, faith is a gift of the Holy Spirit. It must be, if it is a power capable of moving mountains.

2 Corinthians

1:24—"Not that we lord it over your faith, but we are fellow workers for your joy; for you stand by faith."

Faith is the means of standing, or the condition in which one stands.[7] As much as one may regard this statement as a claim by the believer to endure by virtue of his own faith, it is equally valid to understand this phrase

---

5. See also Gal 5:6.

6. See Matt 17:20.

7. See also Rom 4:20 and 11:20 below.

as conveying the thought that it is the power of faith that holds one up and enables one to stand.

13:5—"*Examine each other if you are in the faith, test each other. Or, do you not realize yourselves that Jesus Christ is in you? Unless you fail the test.*"

If ἐν τῇ πίστεως is a mystical phrase akin to ἐν Χριστῷ, then we may have another instance in which faith is the sphere of influence or condition within which a person exists, and not a capacity of the individual. St. Paul could be saying that being in the faith is a condition that comes from Christ being in or among the Corinthians. If so, then faith cannot be claimed to be under the control of the Corinthians. Rather, they are controlled by an outside force.

Romans

1:5 "*through whom we receive grace and apostleship for the obedience of faith among all the nations for the sake of his name.*"

The first mention of the concept of faith in the letter to the Romans occurs in the phrase "obedience of faith" (1:5), which is repeated in Rom 16:26, but nowhere else in ancient literature.[8] This unique Pauline phrase has been variously translated as a genitive of apposition: "the obedience which is faith," or a genitive of source: "obedience from faith," or as an objective genitive: "obedience to faith." The latter possibility (including also the subjective genitive), suffers from the lack of a personal actor. As a genitive of apposition it suffers from Garlington's accusation of a pleonasm.[9]

If, however, the phrase is taken as a genitive of source it signifies that faith produces or is the source of something, in this case obedience.[10] If obedience is produced by faith, then faith must have the power to produce. Unfortunately, the Apostle does not plainly write that faith produces obedience. Perhaps he is being deliberately vague in an effort to appeal to both Jewish and Gentile Christians. Be that as it may, if faith is the source of obedience, as a well is the source of water, it holds within itself a quality that supplies obedience. Rendering the phrase as a genitive of source avoids the theological tangle of equating faith with works as in the appositional translation, while at the same time avoiding any divorce between the two

8. Jewett, *Romans*, 110.

9. Jewett, *Romans*, 110.

10. " . . . or possibly a gen. of source, 'obedience that springs from faith.'" Fitzmyer, *Romans*, 237.

because obedience (works) flows necessarily from faith. Faith and works can never be separated one from another, only distinguished theologically. The relationship between faith and works is more organic than compartmental. In any case, faith in this passage has the ability to produce or supply obedience.

1:16–17—"For I am not ashamed of the gospel, for it is the power of God for salvation to all who believe, both to the Jew first and to the Greek. For the righteousness of God is revealed in it from faith to faith, just as it is written, 'the righteous one will live from faith.'"

The gospel is God's saving power to those who believe. Faith here may be understood as apprehending, absorbing, or receiving that power, but clearly faith has some association with divine power in verse 16. Depending upon how one phrases the words and if one places the emphasis on salvation, Paul means that this divine power produces salvation or somehow serves salvation. Then, in turn, the salvation that God's power has produced is meant for those who believe.

Yet, it may also be the case that this "power of God for salvation" should be understood as a single phrase with the emphasis on "power" and that those who believe are the intended recipients of that power, which is then modified by the prepositional phrase, "of God for salvation." In this way we may understand that Paul remarks on the gift of power to believers.

In verse 17 St. Paul signals his insistence that faith is central to the gospel, righteousness, and life. "From faith to faith" most likely means that the gospel is passed down from believer to believer. But why did the Apostle not write that? Why did he use the objectified noun? Perhaps the answer lies in his use of the phrase from Habakkuk which contains the important phrase "live from faith." Understanding faith as the source of life for the righteous, we recognize that the phrase "from faith to faith" does not merely describe the human exchange of information about God but rather a profound and divine transference of faith in which God is actively at work. The righteousness of God, which is a gift, is revealed from out of faith as a divine power from which those who receive the gift of righteousness are enabled to live.

It is curious that English translators have taken the ἐκ πίστεως phrases and translated them differently. In the first instance ἐκ πίστεως is translated "from faith,"[11] or "through faith."[12] But in the next instance, it

11. NIV.

12. NRSV.

is translated "by faith."[13] In the first instance one may legitimately conclude that faith is the source of something but in the next instance it is translated as an instrument for something. Yet, both phrases are identical and occur in close proximity to each other. Why translate them differently, unless the translators assume that faith is a human product and ability? Rendering "ἐκ πίστεως" as "by faith" would signify that human faith is the tool whereby the righteousness of God is revealed. But such a rendering places too much responsibility upon the individual. After all, God must be the revealer, not the human. I suspect that is why the phrase was translated as a genitive of source instead of an instrumental genitive. But because the translators have misunderstood faith, they have translated the second phrase differently when it should be translated the same way as in the first instance. When translated as "the righteous shall live from faith" the phrase carries the same theological weight as the first phrase instead of relegating it to the realm of human ability. In this way we may understand faith as the source of the Christian life, not a tool to be wielded by the believer. The phrase therefore retains its divine connotation as in the first instance.

Reading 1:16–17 in this fashion leads us to realize that St. Paul is not speaking of a human chain of communication when he mentions "from faith to faith" or a human capacity when he quotes Habakkuk's "live from faith." Rather, he is expressing the mysterious transference of energy from God to humans in the form of faith, which animates the life of the Christian.

4:19–20—"And not weakening with respect to faith, though he considered his own body already dead, being about a hundred years old, and the barrenness of Sara's womb, he did not doubt the promise of God through unbelief but was strengthened by faith and gave glory to God."

Abraham was strengthened by faith. Does that mean he strengthened himself? Surely not, for Paul is trying to make the point that Abraham's human existence was weak, and earlier had said that Abraham did not work, but believed.[14] The Apostle cannot mean that Abraham's self-generated, human faith kept him going, since that would contradict the essential component of his theology of grace, which he has been at pains to explain in chapter 4. Because Abraham is a powerful example of God's gracious salvation and man's inability to achieve that salvation, St. Paul cannot be so inconsistent as to express the view that a man's faith strengthened him as though he were able to pull himself up by his own spiritual bootstraps.

13. Both NIV and NRSV.
14. Rom 4:5.

Instead, the Apostle is emphasizing once again that faith is the power that strengthens not only Abraham but all believers because faith is the power of God in a person's life.[15]

11:20—"True. They were cut off by unbelief, but you stand by faith. Do not think with pride, but with fear."

This passage expresses a similar thought as Rom 4:20, above. Faith enables Christians to stand. But they cannot be proud of this faith. Rather, they must fear and respect God who gives them faith. If that is so, then they can lay no claim to responsibility for it and therefore cannot consider it a human work. Instead, the Apostle looks upon faith as a power that causes Christians to stand fast.

Philippians

Some may wish to point to Phil 2:12 in an effort to maintain the opinion that faith is neither gift nor divine power, but a human production: "work through your own salvation with fear and trembling."[16] Yet, in the very next verse the Apostle insists that it is God who is at work in the Philippians: "for God is the One who enables in you both to will and to work for his good pleasure." The word "γάρ" is the crucial word, for it signifies the reason why Paul may command the Philippians to "work out" their own salvation. He does not mean to say that the Philippians are responsible for their own salvation or that they must strive to achieve or produce that salvation. Instead of translating κατεργάζεσθε as "work out" in the sense of accomplish or achieve, we could very easily translate it as "work through" (κατά with the accusative is often translated "through") in the sense of following through, exhibiting or living out one's salvation in life. Often St. Paul insists that humans are incapable of their own salvation and that whatever salvation they have is pure gift.[17] Therefore, Paul cannot mean here that the Philippians or any other Christian has the responsibility for his or her own

15. St. Paul expresses a similar sentiment in 1 Cor 15:10: "But by the grace of God I am what I am, and his grace toward me was not in vain. But, I worked harder than any of them, though it was not I, but the grace of God that is with me." Here Paul boasts of his hard work, but immediately vacates the boast by insisting that he was not the one working, but rather it was the grace of God that has done the work. Thus, Paul again describes human action that is powered by the divine.

16. This sentiment was pointed out to me by my doctor father, Paul J. Achtemeier, in a personal correspondence.

17. For example: Gal 3:1–3; Rom 3:27–28; 5:12–15; 8:16.

salvation, only that every Christian has the ability because God has granted it. Moreover, in this case, ability is not responsibility, for it is God who is at work within the Philippians, not they themselves. It is God who supplies the will and the work, not the person. That is why Paul may demand that the Philippians work through their salvation or anything else for that matter, because he knows that it is God who does the working and also gives the will to work within the Christian.

Ability does not constitute responsibility any more than the act of breathing constitutes responsibility for life. If the Philippians are able to work out anything toward their salvation they cannot claim any boast or responsibility for that since the engine, the force, the will and ability to do such work is actually God's.

The word, ʽο ἐνεργῶν, is reminiscent of Gal 2:8 where Paul speaks of himself and Peter being "enabled" to preach the gospel. It also echoes the same sentiment from 2 Cor 3:5 in which Paul claims no competence of his own, only that which comes from God. 1 Cor 4:7 expresses the same principle of passive reception. It would seem then that the Apostle is quite deliberate in his insistence that whatever Christians may possess in the way of abilities and talents and however much St. Paul may exhort his listeners to this or that behavior, it is always God who provides the ability and will to do what is good, so that the believer is never on his or her own but always supplied by the Lord with whatever is necessary to live the Christian life. This necessarily includes faith as the essential condition upon which that life is built.

How then may we reconcile the obvious syntactical difficulty of the language of faith which indicates that "I," "you," or "we" believe on the one hand, and the claim that faith is a gift of God on the other? The poverty of our language inclines many to think that believers are the ones who have manufactured faith because the language drives many to that conclusion. Yet, the Pauline conclusion that salvation, faith, and even suffering are all gifts of God argues against any thought that believers, even in small measure, are responsible for their own faith and salvation.

The answer is in this verse in Philippians: that God is at work within the believer to produce salvation.[18] He labors within each individual Christian, and it is this toiling of the divine that produces faith and salvation. Christians may therefore confidently say and write that "we" believe because God has and continues to give them that ability. But they may not

18. Paul expresses a similar thought in Rom 8:9–11.

thereby claim any responsibility for salvation, since it is not they who supply the ability, but God.

Moreover, and this is crucial, it is a continual working within the person. The Apostle does not write in the aorist, but in the present tense. This means that he intends to convey a continual working of the divine within the Philippians and not a momentary, singular event that is never repeated. Rather, as we have seen time and again in St. Paul's letters, he regards the activity of Christ in his life as an ongoing power or force that continues to exert its energy throughout his life and the life of his congregations.

The New Life of Faith

The power of faith gave St. Paul a new life. It transformed him that day on the road to Damascus and continued to do so all his life. The faith of St. Paul has a transformative effect on the individual and gives the believer a new existence.

Galatians 2:20—"But I no longer live, Christ lives in me. The life I now live in the flesh I live in faith to the Son of God who loved me and gave himself up for me. I do not annul the grace of God, for if righteousness is through law then Christ died for nothing."

The NRSV translates Gal 2:20 as, "And the life I now live in the flesh, I live by faith in the Son of God." The ESV and NIV also use the phrase "by faith" to translate the Greek phrase ἐν πίστει. Hanz Dieter Betz, however, in his Hermeneia commentary, translates the phrase "in the faith."[19] In addition, C. F. D. Moule mentions a "sphere of faith" when writing about πίστις followed by ἐν in Paul's epistles.[20] Perhaps if we understood faith as a sphere of influence; as something in which a person may live even while in the body, it would open up a perspective on faith closer to the Apostle's than the idea of faith as a human work. Faith, understood in this way, is like the air we breathe or the arena in which we live. It is a substance or condition in which we find ourselves, not something that we control, but something that provides us with life. If so, St. Paul expresses in this verse the thought that his life is lived within the sphere of faith—a sphere of influence determined not by the individual, but by Christ. Life in faith is life in Christ who lives in the believer. This fits well with the idea that one is made

19. Betz, *Galatians*, 124.

20. Moule, *Idiom Book*, 81. See also Schliesser, who writes of faith as a "Machtsphäre" above p. 54.

righteous "from" faith; that one draws one's righteousness from faith as one draws breath from the air that surrounds a person.[21]

This is a concept that cannot be reduced to lexical definitions, grammar, or syntax. It is not explicable in rational terms, but is rather an unfathomable confession. The Apostle is expressing a mystical relationship that defies human understanding but does so in a manner that signals a certain perspective that contradicts any thought of human responsibility for life, salvation, or faith. Any attempt to relegate faith under the power of the person comes to ruin in this verse. Rather, faith, in this context, is a life-altering, transformative condition.

Galatians 3:11–12—"Because it is evident that in law no one is righteoused before God, because "the righteous one will live from faith." But the law is not from faith, but "the one who does them will live in them."

To live from faith is to exist because of something else. It is to take not only one's energy and capacity but one's motivation for living, from faith. Faith animates and is the source of life. Paul is not writing that a human capacity supplies life, but that when faith comes to a person, that faith brings life with it.

The law is also a source of power, but of a different type. That power is coercive, not transformative. One obeys out of fear and/or the hope of reward. Faith, on the other hand, is the source of willing obedience, so that obedience is no longer an external compulsion but an inner motive. The works of law can never be a source of life for Paul, only the result of a faith-filled life. Faith is the source, obedience is the end result.

Or, as Paul writes in Gal 6:15: "For neither circumcision counts for anything, nor uncircumcision, but a new creation." Here is the point being made clearly that human activity, whatever form it may take, is not what matters. Something else is far more important and profound: the remaking, refashioning, and recreation of the person. To be created anew requires nothing less than death and resurrection by the power of God. That cannot be done through human agency or activity but only through the transforming gift of faith in a person's life. The faith of St. Paul is a divine transformative gift. As such it is not a separate entity manufactured by the human being with or without the "assistance" of God, but it is God in a person's life busily transforming that life from one of death to a life truly lived from faith that results in love and salvation.

---

21. See also 1 Cor 16:13 in which the Apostle writes of standing firm "in faith."

In Gal 6:14–15 the Apostle ends his combative letter with a profound truth that he hopes the Galatians will take to heart. If he has not been successful in persuading them to his theological point of view by making clear the difference between what he had originally taught them and what they had subsequently accepted, then perhaps this final point would suffice to bring them to their senses. They need a new life, different from the old in a way that cannot be comprehended by the old. This new life is made possible, not by human effort, but by the death of Jesus Christ, through whom Paul is dead to the world and the world dead to him. Only through death can new life come. This new life is what the Apostle has been aiming at all through the letter with his arguments about the law, faith, Abraham, circumcision, freedom, the fruits of the Spirit, etc. But it is faith that is the central theme, sounded in his precis of the letter at the end of chapter two[22] and it is the subject of faith that he presses home with his example of Abraham. All of that now culminates in this last morsel of wisdom, that new life, new creation, is the goal of Christ and the crucifixion. Faith in Christ, for Paul, issues in new life. But that life is hidden with Christ and cannot be seen with the naked eye and so must be believed. It is a new life in faith that St. Paul proclaims, one that is true and lasting, but a new life that can only be granted by the power of faith.

Conclusion

The Apostle regards faith as something that works through love as a power for good. He can characterize faith as a power that has the ability to move mountains. Such power cannot come from the human being. He links faith with the power of God and maintains that Abraham was strengthened by faith. Faith is something that comes to a person, not something to which a person comes. It is the very work of God in the believer.

Wilhelm Bousset and Adolf Deissman recognized long ago that faith was an energy and a power.[23] Though he does not do so in describing human faith, Richard Hays labels the faith of Christ as power.[24] Martin Luther praises faith as "living, busy, [and] active."[25] Adolf Schlatter wrote that faith

---

22. Gal 2:15–21.

23. See above p. 10.

24. See above p. 16. See also Hung-Sik, above p. 41.

25. See above p. 44.

is grounded in God's power.[26] Udo Schnelle describes faith as a "life-giving power."[27] Benjamin Schliesser regards faith as a sphere of power.[28] The link between faith and power therefore is nothing new in New Testament scholarship. But it is perhaps a much neglected view that warrants more than a passing mention.

The Philippians passage is instructive for the way St. Paul regards how faith works within the Christian individual and community. It is God Himself working within the person to give that person the will to live for God's purposes. It is the Almighty who grants each believer not only the will but the power to perform God's will. God apportions faith to each as he wills, but the gift of faith that he gives is not a singular event in time. It is a constant and continual working of God within each person to give that person the ongoing will to believe and to live that faith. Because this gift is never disconnected from the *Giver* and because it is continuous in its granting, the Christian abides and lives within the sphere of God's influence and energy. As the Apostle stated in Gal 2:20, "It is not I who live, but Christ who lives in me," and does so from faith.

For St. Paul, the person is transformed by the working of God into a believer who not only agrees with the transformation but actively seeks to live out that transformation in one's own life. This faith is authentic and real not because it is a "free verdict of the human heart," but precisely because it is not. Authentic faith cannot depend upon the human being for its integrity. The human being is not reliable enough to maintain a saving faith that warrants God's approval. Doubt constantly enters the human heart because finite creatures are incapable of grasping the infinite. But the infinite may grasp the finite and recreate it.

Some will complain that such a situation means that people are mere puppets being pulled about on stage by an unseen hand. Not for St. Paul. If he considered people mere puppets in God's control with no will of their own, he would not have told the Philippians that God gives them a new will and energizes them to do His work. Like any good puppeteer he would have kept that secret. But he did not! Not only that but he admonishes his churches numerous times and upbraids them for disobeying God and falling short of divine expectations.[29] The Apostle time and again exhorts his

---

26. See above p. 46.

27. See above p. 50.

28. "Machtsphäre." See above p. 54.

29. 1 Corinthians is replete with such exhortations.

brothers and sisters in Christ to live lives of obedient service. By such words the Apostle is overtly using the means that God has given him to change the hearts and minds of his listeners. Moreover, they are consciously aware of what he is doing and nothing is done in secret or in an underhanded manner (2 Cor 4:2). The transformation which the human being experiences to become a believer is mysterious but not secret. The person may not realize the point at which he or she becomes a believer, but at no point is the person unconscious of the possibility that faith could happen. When a person hears the name of Jesus or listens to someone speak about him or perhaps reads the New Testament, that person is fully aware of what is being said, heard, and read and consciously aware of the possibility of faith.

The Apostle's letters are one-sided conversations of which the other side remains hidden. We do not know what he initially preached to his congregations or how he told them of the advent of faith. Is this why there is no extended discussion in his letters on the origin of faith? Could it be that he had addressed that issue effectively in his congregations and only needed to remind his listeners occasionally and tangentially of what he had said previously? That would account for the few times he plainly characterizes faith as a powerful gift and why it is necessary to delve deeply into his words to identify that characterization.

When we do investigate carefully we find that the faith of St. Paul is a faith in God and Christ that is a powerful, ongoing gift of the Holy Spirit in a person's life, which alters that person's life dramatically. For Paul the Apostle, life as a believer is a union with Christ who lives in him and in whom Paul lives. This new life is bestowed upon him through the working of the Holy Spirit who also works in others to effect the same transformation of new life in which the person actually does believe because that person has been transformed into a believer by the power of God. Therefore, St. Paul may write that one actually does believe without denying the fact that such belief is a gift. Faith as an act of the human being comes about because the human being is given that capacity, not because the individual produced that capacity by oneself. Faith as power is the key to understanding this transformation. If faith were merely an attitude or human decision, it would not have the ability to change the person, for it would come from the person. A power beyond the person is needed to change that person dramatically and authentically. This, God does with faith.

In this way we should not understand human faith as a separate act divorced from God or a separate category of thought or decision as though it were a discreet attitude that constitutes human response to a divine activity. Rather, it is divine activity within the believer that reforms and remakes the person. Too many scholars have uncritically assumed that faith is a separate responsive action of the human being apart from the divine. If, however, we read St. Paul's letters in the fashion suggested here, then we may safely and appropriately emphasize both the divine gift of faith and the fact that "we believe." But the latter statement can never be a ground for boasting because the fact of believing is only possible with the power of the divine gift within the life of the believer.

7

The Faith of St. Paul

Ὥστε εἴ τις ἐν Χριστῷ καινὴ κτίσις[1]

THE FAITH OF ST. Paul is not a quality, condition or ability originating with the human being. It is a transformative gift of divine power.

Yet, the Apostle writes plainly and consistently that people do believe.[2] Scholars have assumed that there are two dimensions to redemption and salvation, one divine and one human, and that these are separate, like different pieces in a machine that cooperate with one another to produce a single effect. God's grace, they say, must be responded to by human faith, and so the two pieces fit together to produce salvation. Even among scholars who acknowledge faith as a gift, they too think of it mechanistically as a human act separate from the divine.

It is this mechanistic view that has, in part, obscured the true nature of faith in St. Paul's letters. He does not view faith as a discreet dialectical component that operates as a human cog in a larger machine completely separate from the inventor. His view is more organic. The Apostle's faith is something that God works in people to produce the will and work for his own good pleasure.[3] When the Spirit gives his gifts those gifts are truly

---

1. 2 Cor 5:17.
2. See above p. 58.
3. Phil 2:12–13.

performed by the recipients.[4] St. Paul's faith, just as the other gifts of the Spirit, is not a separate spiritual component that when once given is out of the control of the *Giver*. Rather, it is a continuous gift through the Word that is never separate from the *One* who gives it.[5]

This gift requires prior approval of the Almighty.[6] It is revealed in time with the coming of Christ.[7] Faith, therefore, has an external source apart from the human being and cannot be considered a product of human wisdom or understanding.[8] For St. Paul, it is the external Word of the gospel that delivers this powerful gift.[9] Just as righteousness and salvation are gifts of God's grace,[10] so too must be faith, the avenue of such gifts.[11] When the Apostle writes that one is made righteous from faith, he writes of faith as a source, not an instrument to be wielded by the person.[12] This is why he used the passage from Habakkuk in the manner he did, in order to demonstrate that one does not use faith for one's life as one uses a tool, but that one derives one's life from faith as a source of divine blessing.[13]

This divine gift is not static, but is active in a person's life. Faith produces love[14] and works through love.[15] Faith has the power to move mountains.[16] It empowered Abraham and enables Christians to stand.[17] It results in obedience.[18] This powerful gift not only supplies certain abilities

---

4. 1 Cor 12:6–9; Gal 5:22–23.

5. Gal 2:20; 3:5 convey the thought of a life that is lived continuously in Christ through the constant hearing of the Word. See also Phil 2:12.

6. 1 Thess 2:4.

7. Gal 3:22–27.

8. 1 Cor 1:21.

9. Rom 10:14–17.

10. Rom 3:24.

11. Phil 3:9; Gal 2:16.

12. Gal 2:16.

13. Rom 1:17.

14. 1 Thess 1:3.

15. Gal 3:5.

16. 1 Cor 13:2.

17. Rom 4:19–20; 2 Cor 1:24.

18. Rom 1:5 (16:26).

necessary for the believer but it constitutes the believer's whole life.[19] A new creation is the final result.[20]

The faith of St. Paul is a transformative gift of divine power that continuously bestows new life through the word of Christ.

Theological Ramifications

The theological ramifications of this study are significant for the debate between those who claim participation in Christ as the central theme of Pauline theology and those who argue for justification or righteousness by faith as the center. If we follow this present study to its logical conclusion, the two are, in fact, one. Participation in Christ is justification by faith. At the same time, the seeming contradiction of faith as gift and faith as human act is also remedied. Consequently, the *Pistis Christou* debate becomes moot.

Justification by Faith and Being in Christ

E. P. Sanders recognized that righteousness by faith and participation in Christ amounted to the same thing.[21] But because he regards faith as a human work and thinks mechanistically about righteousness as something prior to life in Christ, he is unable to combine the two emphases effectively.[22] Jouette Bassler intriguingly approaches a solution when she writes, "If faith involves participation in Christ, the two lines of thought merge into one."[23] Douglas Campbell attempts something similar when he asserts that faith encompasses ethics, which provides a theological bridge to participation in Christ.[24] N. T. Wright also wishes to combine righteousness by faith and participation in Christ, but only suggests a possible avenue by which it might be accomplished.

There is, therefore, in some scholars the awareness and desire to link righteousness/justification by faith and being-in-Christ/participation in

---

19. Gal 2:20.

20. Gal 6:15.

21. See above, p. 4.

22. Sanders, *Paul and Palestinian Judaism*, 506–7, where he lays out the reasons why righteousness cannot be the "gateway to life."

23. Bassler, *Navigating Paul*, 32.

24. See above p. 52.

Christ. It is as though they sense the need to accomplish the unity, but cannot see their way to doing so.

Albert Schweitzer first drove a wedge between the two emphases because he could not conceive of faith as a gift of God. He assumed, without argument, that faith was a human work. Because of this he was blind to the realization that being in Christ meant faith in Christ. St. Paul knew that when a person is changed into a believer by the gift of faith, that person was in Christ and Christ in that person.[25] There is absolutely no reason to oppose participation in Christ to justification by faith since the two emphases are unified in the gift of faith, which is the divine power to alter human lives and cause them to live a new life.

Adolf Deissmann understood this when he described faith as union with God and something that does not precede justification but *is* the "experience of justification."[26] Schweitzer was more interested in the contextual influences on St. Paul's thinking rather than the intersection between faith and union with Christ, due to his misunderstanding of St. Paul's faith. Schweitzer briefly comments on Deissmann's connecting of faith and union with Christ: "In what way the belief in the Messiahship of Jesus attained on the Damascus road immediately grew into a mysticism of Being-in-Christ Deissmann does not attempt to explain. He does not seem to have any consciousness of the difference between the two convictions."[27] Schweitzer did not fathom Deissmann's connection between the two because he had a diametrically opposite view of faith. For Deissmann, faith was a living gift. For Schweitzer, it was only a firmly held point of view. It is no wonder that Schweitzer could not grasp the intimate connection between faith and being-in-Christ, and could not understand those who did.

Schweitzer was correct about Paul's mysticism (that St. Paul's thought processes extended to a plane beyond the mundane), but wrong about its complexion. The Apostle was very much a mystic, and if we were to encounter him today we would most likely label him a religious fanatic. But had Schweitzer properly understood the nature of Paul's faith, he would have been able to understand how it was that ethics was tied up with justification because faith, which supplies justification also produces and works through love as a divine power within the believer's life. As St. Paul clearly says in Gal 2:20: Faith is life in Christ.

25. Gal 2:20.
26. Deissmann, *St. Paul*, 146–47.
27. Schweitzer, *Mysticism*, 35.

Faith in Christ, therefore, is being in Christ, and Christ in the believer. Because faith is God's power in a person's life it creates a new person in whom Christ takes up residence and transforms, indeed, recreates the person. The Christian does not "participate" in Christ as though the Christian life were a sporting event in which one may participate as long as one likes.[28] The faith of St. Paul is a transformative gift of divine power that involves the entire Christian (and the whole Christ!).

Faith as Gift and Act

It follows from the preceding observations that the question of how faith can be a divine gift and at the same time an activity of the human being is answered. The fruits or manifestations of the Spirit are listed in Gal 5 and 1 Cor 12.[29] These gifts are abilities that are clearly exercised by people, one of which is faith. When St. Paul lists such gifts he is plainly expressing the idea that the person is enabled to perform the gifts, not merely possess them. The same is true with faith. It is a gift that God gives and that gift is meant to be performed, demonstrated, practiced, and enacted by the individuals. Because faith is a transformative gift of divine power that recreates the person, thus making that person into a believer, one may confidently assert that one does believe, but without any attendant boasting as though such faith were self-engendered.

The difficulty we face is in the language we use to describe this mysterious phenomenon. To describe something as a human act seems as though we were asserting human responsibility or boasting. But this is something the Apostle categorically rejects.[30] Yet, he can write that people, in fact, believe because he regards faith not as a separate human action apart from God but one that resides within the sphere of influence of the creative word of God and the gift of faith.[31] Indeed, St. Paul writes in Philippians of God

---

28. The phrase "participation in Christ" has always struck me as wholly inadequate and diminutive of the union of Christ and the believer. Schweitzer's "Being-in-Christ" is far better. The believer needs the whole Christ, not just a "part" of him.

29. Gal 5:22–23; 1 Cor 12:7–11.

30. Rom 3:27.

31. Here Moule's and Schliesser's observations of faith as a sphere of influence or Machtshpäre are helpful. See p. 76, n. 13.

himself working in people to produce what God desires.[32] The gift of faith is the act of faith in St. Paul's theology.

This dual or dialectical way of thinking is characteristic of the Apostle who can also claim that believers have known and have been known by God,[33] have seized and have been seized by Christ,[34] or that those who weep or rejoice do so as though they were not.[35] The deeply troubling condition of St. Paul's inner self is confusingly related in Romans 7 where he states that though he may wish to do good, he cannot accomplish it because of the dual nature of his existence.[36] St. Paul may therefore hold two seemingly disparate views in a single thought and hold them tightly together as a single thought. It is when we try to split that single thought and over-analyze the Apostle's thinking by separating the two halves that we discover we have been hoisted by our own petard![37] Instead of trying to separate such thoughts and emphasizing one aspect over the other (righteousness over faith/faith over righteousness; the act of faith over the gift of faith/the gift over the act) we should rather hold them in tension and allow the single thought to stand on its own two legs.[38]

When one properly understands faith as a transformative gift of divine power, one may also overcome the notion that justification by faith (as a judicial or juridical concept) and faith as an existential reality are in conflict with one another. Again, they are one. Justification by faith is not merely a concept that describes a detached and forensic act of God that is declared in the heavens or written in a book without the person even present. On the contrary, justification by faith is an intimately personal event that seeks to describe the advent of faith deep within one's life. Since faith is divine power, and since faith is a gift of transformation, then justification by faith is the declaration that one's life has been profoundly altered in truth as an existential reality.

32. 2:12.

33. Gal 4:9.

34. Phil 3:12.

35. 1 Cor 7:30.

36. Rom 7:18–25.

37. *Pace* Shakespeare!

38. Thanks to my father, Roy A. Harrisville Jr., for this observation.

Πίστις Χριστοῦ

The current debate over the πίστις Χριτοῦ issue is also impacted by the understanding of faith as a gift. When St. Paul contrasts faith and works, he is not placing in opposition two different kinds of human work.[39] Rather, he is pointing out that works of the law as human efforts to achieve or maintain God's approval have nothing to do with the gift of faith. It is only because Richard Hays could not conceive of faith as a gift that he thought he was compelled to offer up a creative reading of an opposition that he misunderstood. There is no reason in this case to translate ἡ πίστις as faithfulness and apply that to Jesus of Nazareth in order to overcome the mistaken notion that St. Paul was opposing two forms of human works. When one understands that the faith of St. Paul is a gift, the opposition becomes clear and requires no novel interpretation. As Moises Silva once remarked, if faith is a gift "then the main (theological) motivation for arguing that πίστις Ἰησοῦ Χριστοῦ refers to Christ's own faith(fullness) turns out to be a phantom."[40]

Conclusion

Immanuel Kant was no friend of the Christian faith. Yet, he understood the profound nature of that faith when he wrote that if there existed a faith that was so powerful it could refashion a person "from the ground up," it would spell the "dance of death" of human reason.[41] The Apostle Paul well knew the limits of human reason and also knew the power of the life that encountered him on the road to Damascus.[42] That is why he used the language of new creation,[43] of death and life,[44] and of rebirth.[45] He did so because he knew and believed that the Christian's existence was not a mere improvement of one's previous life, but an altogether new life.

This life was not of the Apostle's own making. It was a gift. It changed him from Saul, the persecutor of the Church, to St. Paul, the champion

---

39. As does Richard Hays, above on p. 17.
40. Silva, "Faith Versus Works," 234.
41. Kant, *Die Religion*, 111.
42. Acts 9:4.
43. Gal 6:15.
44. Rom 6:3–4.
45. Rom 6:11.

of the faith he had once despised.[46] An obligation was laid upon him,[47] a slavery he could not escape.[48] He was energized by someone else for service to this new life in order to carry out his ministry[49] and he never boasted of any of it.[50] Such a life could not have come from within himself, nor from within any human being. No amount of mental or spiritual exercise could hope to attain the goal of righteousness before a holy God. Yet, if that righteousness were bestowed upon the person, given to the person as a divine gift, then not only could real transformation take place within the person, but a whole new life could emerge from the ashes of the old. This new life was not of the Apostle's making, nor did it even belong to him. Because this new life was neither his possession nor his doing, he could not lay claim to any credit or boast. For who can boast of a gift? And yet, this new life was genuinely and truly his, just as it was meant to be by the *Giver*.

It was this new life that St. Paul proclaimed to his congregations time and again, and would have continued to do so until old age, had his life not been cut short in Rome. He had no choice in the matter, for an external obligation had been laid upon him,[51] a compulsion that came not from his old life, but from his new. It was the gift of this new life that compelled the Apostle to his mission and that same divine gift that proves itself effective in every life it transforms.

---

46. Gal 2:23.

47. 1 Cor 9:16.

48. The Apostle often refers to himself as a slave or servant of Christ. Rom 1:1, etc.

49. Gal 2:8.

50. Phil 3:1–7.

51. 1 Cor 9:16.

Bibliography

The American Heritage Dictionary of the English Language. Fourth Edition. Boston: Houghton Mifflin Company, 2000.

Barclay, John M. G. "Grace and the Transformation of Agency in Christ." In *Redefining First-Century Jewish and Christian Identities: Essays in Honor of Ed Parish Sanders*, edited by Fabian E. Udoh with Susannah Heschel, Mark Chancey, and Gregory Tatum, 372–89. Notre Dame, IN: University of Notre Dame Press, 2008.

Barth, Gerhard. πίστις, εως, ἡ. In *Exegetisches Wörterbuch zum Neuen Testament*, Horst Balz/Gerhard Schneider (Hrsg.), Band III, 216–31. Zweite, verbesserte Auflage mit Literatur-Nachträgen. Stuttgart: Kohlhammer, 1992.

Bassler, Jouette. *Navigating Paul: An Introduction to Key Theological Concepts.* Louisville: Westminster John Knox, 2007.

Bauer, Walter, Frederick W. Danker, W. F. Arndt, and F. W. Gingrich. *Greek-English Lexicon of the New Testament and Other Early Christian Literature.* 3rd ed. Chicago: University of Chicago Press, 2000.

Becker, Jürgen. *Paul: Apostle to the Gentiles.* Translated by O. C. Dean, Jr. Louisville: Westminster/John Knox, 1993.

Betz, Hans Dieter. *Galatians: A Commentary on Paul's Letter to the Churches in Galatia.* Hermeneia. Philadelphia: Fortress, 1979.

Die Bibel. Nach der Übersetzung Martin Luthers. Stuttgart: Deutsche Bibelgesellschaft, 1984.

Blass, Friedrich, and Albert Debrunner. *A Greek Grammar of the New Testament and Other Early Christian Literature.* Translated and revised by Robert W. Funk. Chicago: University of Chicago Press, 1961.

Bornkamm, Günther. *Paul.* Translated by D. M. G. Stalker. New York: Harper & Row, 1971.

Bousset, Wilhelm. *Kyrios Christos: A History of the Belief in Christ from the Beginnings of Christianity to Irenaeus.* Translated by John E. Steely. Nashville: Abingdon, 1970.

Brown, Francis, S. R. Driver, and Charles A. Briggs. *Hebrew and English Lexicon of the Old Testament.* Oxford: Clarendon, 1907.

Bultmann, Rudolf. "III. πίστις and πιστεύω in Paul." In πιστεύω, πίστις, κτλ, in vol. 4 of *Theological Dictionary of the New Testament*, edited by G. Friedrich, translated and edited by Geoffrey W. Bromiley, 217–22. Grand Rapids: Eerdmans, 1968.

Calvin, John. *Acts of the Council of Trent With Its Antidote.* The Comprehensive John Calvin Collection. Ages Digital Library, 1998.

Bibliography

———. *Commentary on Ezekiel.* The Comprehensive John Calvin Collection. Ages Digital Library, 1998.

———. *Institutes of the Christian Religion.* Edited by John T. McNeill; translated by Ford Lewis Battles. 2 vols. Philadelphia: Westminster, 1960.

Campbell, Douglas A. "Participation and Faith in Paul." In *"In Christ" in Paul: Explorations in Paul's Theology of Union and Participation,* edited by Michael J. Thate, Kevin J. Vanhoozer, and Constantine R. Campbell, 37–60. Wissenschaftliche Untersuchungen zum Neuen Testament, 2.Reihe, 384. Tübingen: Mohr Siebeck, 2014.

Catechism of the Catholic Church. http://www.vatican.va/archive/ccc_css/archive/catechism/p1s1c3a1.htm.

Conzelmann, Hans. *1 Corinthians: A Commentary on the First Epistle to the Corinthians.* Translated by James W. Leitch; edited by George W. MacRae. Hermeneia. Philadelphia: Fortress, 1975.

Dana, H. E., and Julius R. Mantey. *A Manual Grammar of the Greek New Testament.* New York: MacMillan, 1955.

Deissmann, Adolf. *St. Paul: A Study in Social and Religious History.* Translated by Lionel R. M. Strachman. Eugene, OR: Wipf & Stock, 2004.

Dunn, James D. G. *The Theology of Paul the Apostle.* Grand Rapids: Eerdmans, 1998.

Elliott, Mark W. "Πίστις Χριστοῦ in the Church Fathers and Beyond." In *Faith of Jesus Christ: Exegetical, Biblical, and Theological Studies,* edited by Michael F. Bird and Preston M. Sprinkle 277–89. Massachusetts: Hendrickson, 2009.

Fitzmyer, Joseph A. *Romans: A New Translation with Introduction and Commentary.* The Anchor Bible. New York: Doubleday, 1993.

Fowl, Stephen E. *Philippians.* The Two Horizons New Testament Commentary. Grand Rapids: Eerdmans, 2005.

Francis, Pope. *Encyclical Letter LUMEN FIDEI of the Supreme Pontiff Francis to the Bishops, Priests and Deacons Consecrated Persons and the Lay Faithful on Faith.* New York: Image, 2013.

Friedrich, Gerhard. "Glaube und Verkündigung bei Paulus." In *Glaube im Neuen Testament: Studien zu Ehren von Hermann Binder anläßlich seines 70. Geburtstags,* edited by Ferdinand Hahn and Hans Klein, et al., 93–113. Biblisch-Theologische Studien 7. Neukirchen-Vluyn: Neukirchener Verlag des Erziehungsvereins, 1982.

Gorman, Michael J. *Becoming the Gospel: Paul, Participation, and Mission.* The Gospel and Our Culture series. Grand Rapids: Eerdmans, 2015.

Harrisville, Roy A. *1 Corinthians.* ACNT. Minneapolis: Augsburg, 1987.

Harrisville, Roy A., III. *The Figure of Abraham in the Epistles of St. Paul: In the Footsteps of Abraham.* San Francisco: Mellen Research University Press, 1992.

———. "ΠΙΣΤΙΣ ΧΡΙΣΤΟΥ: Witness of the Fathers." *NovT* 36 (1994) 233–41.

Hays, Richard B. *The Faith of Jesus Christ: The Narrative Substructure of Galatians 3:1–4:11.* 2nd ed. Biblical Resource Series. Grand Rapids: Eerdmans, 2002.

———. "What Is 'Real Participation in Christ'? A Dialogue with E. P. Sanders on Pauline Soteriology." In *Redefining First-Century Jewish and Christian Identities: Essays in Honor of Ed Parish Sanders,* edited by Fabian E. Udoh with Susannah Heschel, Mark Chancey, and Gregory Tatum, 336–51. Indiana: University of Notre Dame Press, 2008.

Hermisson, Hans-Jürgen, and Eduard Lohse. *Faith.* Translated by Douglas W. Stott. Biblical Encounters Series. Nashville: Abingdon, 1981.

Hooker, Morna D. "Another Look at Pistis Christou." *SJT* 69 (2016) 46–62.

Bibliography

————. "ΠΙΣΤΙΣ ΧΡΙΣΤΟΥ." NTS 35 (1989) 321–42.

Hung-Sik, Choi. "ΠΙΣΤΙΣ in Galatians 5:5–6: Neglected Evidence for the Faithfulness of Christ." JBL 124 (2005) 467–90.

Jewett, Robert. *Romans: A Commentary.* Edited by Eldon J. Epp. Hermeneia. Philadelphia: Fortress, 2007.

Kant, Immanuel. *Die Religion innerhalb der Grenzen der bloßen Vernunft.* 4. Auflage. Durchgesehener Neusatz mit einer Biographie des Autors bearbeitet und eingerichtet von Michael Holzinger. Berliner Ausgabe, 2016.

————. *Religion within the Boundaries of Mere Reason and Other Writings.* Translated and edited by Allen Wood and George Di Giovanni. Cambridge: Cambridge University Press, 1998.

Käsemann, Ernst. *New Testament Questions of Today.* Study Edition. The New Testament Library. London: SCM, 1969.

————. *On Being a Disciple of the Crucified Nazarene: Unpublished Lectures and Sermons.* Edited by Rudolf Landau; translated by Roy A. Harrisville. Grand Rapids: Eerdmans, 2010.

————. *Perspectives on Paul.* Philadelphia: Fortress, 1971.

Louw, Johannes P., and Eugene A. Nida, eds. *Greek-English Lexicon of the New Testament Based on Semantic Domains.* 2nd ed. New York: United Bible Societies, 1989.

Luther, Martin. *Introduction to the New Testament.* Vol. 35 of *Luther's Works, Word and Sacrament I,* edited by E. Theodore Bachmann and Helmut T. Lehmann. Philadelphia: Fortress, 1960.

————. *Lectures on Galatians 1535 Chapters 1–4.* Vol. 26 of *Luther's Works.* Saint Louis: Concordia, 1963.

————. *Luther's Works.* The American Edition. Vols. 1–55. Edited by Jaroslav Pelikan and Helmut T. Lehmann. St. Louis: Concordia; Philadelphia: Fortress, 1955–1986. Vols. 58–60, 69, edited by Christopher Boyd Brown. St. Louis: Concordia, 2009–2012.

————. *On Christian Liberty.* Translated by W. A. Lambert; revised by Harold J. Grimm. Minneapolis: Fortress, 2003.

Martyn, J. Louis. *Galatians: A New Translation with Introduction and Commentary.* New York: Doubleday, 1997.

Moule, C. F. D. *An Idiom Book of New Testament Greek.* Cambridge: Cambridge University Press, 1979.

Mundle, Wilhelm. *Der Glaubensbegriff des Paulus: Eine Untersuchung zur Dogmengeschichte des ältesten Christentums.* Darmstadt: Wissenschaftliche Buchgesellschaft, 1977.

Need, Stephen W. *Paul Today: Challenging Readings of Acts and the Epistles.* Essential Inquiries 1. Lanham: Cowley Publications, 2007.

Oden, Thomas C. *The Justification Reader.* Classic Christian Readers series. Grand Rapids: Eerdmans, 2002.

Oxford Classical Dictionary. Edited by Simon Hornblower and Antony Spawforth. 4th ed. Oxford: Oxford University Press, 2012.

Sanders, E. P. *Paul and Palestinian Judaism: A Comparison of Patterns of Religion.* Philadelphia: Fortress, 1977.

————. *Paul, the Law, and the Jewish People.* Minneapolis: Fortress, 1983.

Schlatter, Adolf. *Der Glaube im Neuen Testament.* Vierte Bearbeitung. Stuttgart: Calwer, 1927.

Schliesser, Benjamin. *Abraham's Faith in Romans 4: Paul's Concept of Faith in Light of the History of Reception of Genesis 15:6.* Edited by Jörg Frey. Wissenschaftliche

Untersuchungen zum Neuen Testament—2. Reihe. 224. Tübingen: Mohr Siebeck, 2007.

————. "'Christ-Faith' as an Eschatological Event (Galatians 3.23–26): A 'Third View' on Πίστις Χριστοῦ." JSNT 38 (2016) 277–300.

————. *Was ist Glaube?* Edited by Thomas Schlag, Reiner Anselm, Jörg Frey, and Philipp Stoellger. Paulinische Perspektiven, Theologische Studien, Neue Folge. Zurich: Theologischer Verlag, 2011.

Schnelle, Udo. *Apostle Paul: His Life and Theology.* Translated by M. Eugene Boring. Grand Rapids: Baker Academic, 2003.

Schweitzer, Albert. *The Mysticism of Paul the Apostle.* Translated by William Montgomery. Baltimore: The Johns Hopkins University Press, in association with The Albert Schweitzer Institute for the Humanities, 1998.

————. *Die Mystik des Apostels Paulus.* Zweite, photomechanisch gedruckter Auflage. Tübingen: J.C.B. Mohr (Paul Siebeck), 1954.

Silva, Moisés. "Faith Versus Works of Law in Galatians." In *Justification and Variegated Nomism* Volume 2, *The Paradoxes of Paul,* edited by D. A. Carson, Peter T. O'Brien, and Mark A. Seifrid, 217–48. Grand Rapids: Baker Academic, 2004.

Stendahl, Krister. "The Apostle Paul and the Introspective Conscience of the West." In *Paul Among Jews and Gentiles and Other Essays,* 78–96. Philadelphia: Fortress, 1976.

Stowers, Stanley K. *A Rereading of Romans.* New Haven: Yale University Press, 1994.

————. "What Is 'Pauline Participation in Christ'?" In *Redefining First-Century Jewish and Christian Identities: Essays in Honor of Ed Parish Sanders,* edited by Fabian E. Udoh, Susannah Heschel, Mark Chancey, and Gregory Tatum, 352–71. Indiana: University of Notre Dame Press, 2008.

Stuhlmacher, Peter. *Revisiting Paul's Doctrine of Justification: A Challenge to the New Perspective.* Downers Grove, IL: Intervarsity, 2001.

Wagner, Günther. "The Apostolic Faith According to the New Testament. The Interpretation in the Letters and Later Parts of the New Testament: The Pauline Homologoumena." In *The Roots of Our Common Faith: Faith in the Scriptures and in the Early Church,* edited by Hans-Georg Link, 55–71. Faith and Order Paper No. 119. Geneva: World Council of Churches, 1984.

Watson, Francis. *Paul and the Hermeneutics of Faith.* London: T&T Clark, 2004.

————. *Paul, Judaism and the Gentiles: Beyond the New Perspective.* Revised and expanded ed. Grand Rapids: Eerdmans, 2007.

Westerholm, Stephen. *Perspectives Old and New on Paul: The "Lutheran" Paul and His Critics.* Grand Rapids: Eerdmans, 2004.

————. *Preface to the Study of Paul.* Grand Rapids: Eerdmans, 1997.

————. *Understanding Paul: The Early Christian Worldview of the Letter to the Romans.* 2nd ed. Grand Rapids: Baker Academic. 2004.

Wright, N. T. *Justification: God's Plan & Paul's Vision.* Downers Grove, IL: IVP Academic, 2009.

————. *Paul and the Faithfulness of God.* Book II, Parts III and IV. Christian Origins and the Question of God 4. Minneapolis: Fortress, 2013.

————. *Paul and His Recent Interpreters: Some Contemporary Debates.* Minneapolis: Fortress, 2015.

————. *Paul in Fresh Perspective.* Minneapolis: Fortress, 2005.

Author Index

B

Barclay, John M. G., 5, 107
Barth, Gerhard, 15, 107
Bassler, Jouette, 30–32, 100, 107
Becker, Jürgen, 29–30, 107
Betz, Hans Dieter, 66, 72, 92, 107
Bornkamm, Günther, 46–47, 107
Bousset, Wilhelm, 10–11, 94, 107
Bultmann, Rudolf, xv, 13–15, 30–31,
    49, 66, 84, 107

C

Calvin, John, 44–45, 107–108
Campbell, Douglas A, xv, 52–53, 56,
    100, 108
Catechism of the Catholic Church, xii,
    108

D

Deissmann, Adolf, 10–11, 101, 108
Dunn, James D. G., 16, 31–33, 108

E

Elliott, Mark W, 22, 109

F

Fitzmyer, Joseph A, 87, 108
Pope Francis, xiii–xiv, 108
Fowl, Stephen E., 60, 108
Friedrich, Gerhard, 48–49, 63, 107–8

G

Gorman, Michael J., 53–54, 56, 108

H

Harrisville, Roy A. Jr., ix, 66, 103,
    108–109
Harrisville, Roy A. III, 69, 108
Hays, Richard B., xvi–xvii, 3–5, 16–22,
    24, 54, 62, 72, 94, 104, 108
Hermisson, Hans-Jürgen, 26–27, 108
Hooker, Morna D., 19, 21–22, 31, 66,
    108
Hung-Sik, Choi, 40–42, 94, 109

J

Jewett, Robert, 68, 87, 109

K

Kant, Immanuel, Epigraph, xvii, 104,
    109
Käsemann, Ernst, xv–xvi, 47–48, 56,
    82, 109

L

Lohse, Eduard, 26–27, 108
Luther, Martin, ix, 43–44, 78, 94, 107,
    109

Author Index

M

Martyn, J. Louis, 22–23, 109
Moule, C. F. D., 76, 92, 102, 109
Mundle, Wilhelm, 12–15, 18, 49, 109

N

Need, Stephen W., 28, 109

O

Oden, Thomas C., 33–34, 109

S

Sanders, E. P., xv–xvi, 1–5, 12, 38, 100, 108–10

Schlatter, Adolf, 45–46, 54, 94, 109
Schliesser, Benjamin, 13, 46, 54–56, 73, 76, 92, 95, 102, 109–10
Schnelle, Udo, 50–51, 56, 95, 110
Schweitzer, Albert, xv, 2, 4–12, 18, 21, 53, 62, 101–2, 110
Silva, Moisés, 20, 51–52, 83, 104, 110
Stendahl, Krister, xii, 110
Stowers, Stanley K., 4–5, 28–29, 110
Stuhlmacher, Peter, 49–50, 110

W

Wagner, Günther, 15–16, 27–28, 110
Watson, Francis, 37–40, 55, 110
Westerholm, Stephen, , 35–37, 110
Wright, N. T., xv–xvi, 23–26, 72, 100, 110

Scripture Index

Genesis

15:6   37, 45

Habakkuk

2:4   78

Matthew

17:20   86

John

1:12–13   43

Acts

9:1–19   xii
9:4   104
22:3–21   xii
26:9–20   xii

Romans

1:1–6   38
1:5   xiv, 50, 87, 99
1:6   46
1:8   58
1:12   58
1:16–17   58, 88, 89
1:16   30
1:17   34, 55, 64, 78, 99
3:2–3   58, 61

3:21–22   58, 79
3:24   38, 99
3:25–28   58, 80
3:25   34
3:26   64
3:27–31   54
3:27–28   90
3:27   102
3:30–31   81
4:3–5   58, 69
4:3   58, 45
4:5   89
4:11–14   70
4:11   58
4:14   42
4:16–20   58
4:16   64, 70
4:18   62
4:19–20   89, 99
4:20–22   34
4:20   86, 90
4:21   32
4:24   58
5:1–2   58, 81
5:1   64
5:12–15   90
5:17   36, 79
5:24   58
6:3–4   104
6:8   58, 62
6:11   104
6:16–17   50
7:18–25   103

Romans *(continued)*

8:16	90
8:9–11	91
9:30–33	58
9:30	64
10:4	58
10:6	64
10:8	57
10:9–11	58, 63
10:14–17	38, 58, 75, 99
10:16	50
10:17	50
11:20	86, 90
12:3	52, 68
12:6	69
13:11	58
14:1	58
14:2	58
14:22–23	58, 63
15:13	58
15:18	50
16:19	50
16:26	xiv, 58, 87, 99

1 Corinthians

1:9	57, 58
1:18	46
1:21	58, 73, 99
2:4–5	46, 50
2:5	58, 85
3:5	58, 67
3:17	30
4:2	57, 58
4:7	epigraph, 60, 91
4:15	48
4:17	57, 58
7:25	57, 58
7:30	103
9:16	xii, 105
9:17	63
10:13	57, 58
11:18	57, 58
12	66
12:6–9	67, 99
12:7–11	102
12:8–10	66

13:2	xvii, 85, 99
13:7	57
14:22	58
15:8	xii
15:10	90
15:11	58, 60
15:14	58
15:17	58
15:45	30
15:56	75
16:13	93

2 Corinthians

1:17–22	21
1:18	57
1:24	86, 99
3:5	91
4:2	96
4:6	50
4:13	61
5:7	61
5:14–21	53
5:17	98
6:15	57
8:7	58, 68
10:15	58
11:23–27	40
13:5	87

Galatians

1:13–14	xi
1:13	39
1:14	39
1:23	57
2:15f.	3
2:16	13, 34, 58, 77, 78
2:8–9	85
2:8	91, 105
2:15–21	94
2:16	99
2:20	92, 99, 100, 101
2:23	105
3:1–3	90
3:2–5	80
3:2	50, 75
3:5	75, 84, 99

3:6–9	58
3:9	57, 58
3:11–12	78, 93
3:11	78
3:13	41
3:14	74, 85
3:20	72
3:22	16
3:22–27	58, 72, 99
3:23–26	40
3:23–25	41
3:27	73
4:6	30
4:9	49, 103
5:1	41
5:5–6	85
5:6	41, 86
5:22–23	99, 102
5:22	65, 67
6:10	58
6:14–15	94
6:15	3, 93, 100, 104

Ephesians

2:8	45

Philippians

1:5	36
1:7	36
1:12	36
1:25	57
1:29	36, 49
2:12–13	98
2:12f.	49
2:12	36, 90, 99, 103

2:13	36
2:17	60
2:22	36
2:27	57
3:1–7	105
3:7–9	40
3:8–11	34, 76
3:9	76, 99
3:12	49, 77, 103
4:3	36
4:13	77
4:15	36

1 Thessalonians

1:3	83, 99
1:6–7	58
1:8	59
2:4	71, 99
2:10	59
2:13	59
3:2	59
3:5	59
3:6	59
3:7	59
3:10	73
4:14	59
5:8	73
5:24	57, 58

2 Thessalonians

1:11	84

Philemon

5–6	59